"Really enjoyed reading the [...]
day Christians searching fc [...]
a lifestyle should encourage its readers that prayer is powerful in the
hands of a loving God who has no limitations."
–Rev. Jeff Frost, Campus Pastor, Prayer Track Leader, Eston College

***

"The chapters were thought provoking and helpful in contem-
plating my own prayer life. This is a very powerful book,
because the writer uses real life testimonies that touch the heart."
– Isabel Didreksen

***

Unmasking Myths is a great read for those wanting to grow deeper in
their prayer life. Full of personal stories and perspectives, you will be
drawn into a greater desire to develop your relationship with Jesus. As
that happens, it is impossible for your prayer life to remain where it is.
It must and will develop in a new level of maturity and intimacy with
Jesus.
– Pastor Kenn Parker, National Apostolic Team, Apostolic Church of
Pentecost

***

MaryAnn is a faithful prayer warrior, such a great encourager and a
Jesus role model. I am encouraged by her obedience to do what the
Lord has called her to do . . . First, I like the layout of the stories,
hearing the different experiences of individuals in how they communicate with the Lord and how the Lord speaks to them . . . My eyes
were opened to even more ways God speaks to us and not to put
limits on God. I see how God is so ever present and I can talk with
him anytime, anywhere out loud or in my mind, in a song, or in a
whisper. Second, I appreciated the genuineness of the individuals, and
the simplicity of God when he speaks. Third, one way I know the
Lord speaks to me is through books—books that also give you examples, practical ways to get on the right road, and this book has done
that. Prayer has been a challenge for me, but I am so encouraged to
keep pressing on and communicating with Jesus anywhere, anytime."
– Maria Winkel

***

"E.M. Bounds once said, 'Don't pray for work, prayer is the work.' Prayer is one of the most necessary elements of our spiritual life but least understood. MaryAnn Ward makes the topic accessible while not cutting away the mystery of it. Through anecdotes of many, the power is illustrated. Like biblical miracles the uniqueness of each is left to ponder while the power of individual answers is highlighted. From the spiritually timid to the seasoned there is something for everyone packed in this book."
– Sheila Webster, Life and Book Coach, author of *Reubens Gone*

***

"Wow! Great . . . reading this book, I walked away with a greater understanding, desire and means to prayer. The use of testimony to create this book is so powerful and enjoyable to read. People love to hear true stories about others' experiences; they speaks like no other stories. To see the faithfulness of God, again and again, in people's lives, speaks more than any story that could be imagined. I see this book being used as a daily encouragement as well as a study on prayer."
– Waylon Kardash

***

I never grew up as a Christian—no mentors upon being saved In a way I've taken the "long way" around. My only exposure to prayer has been at church. I really believed prayer had to be formal and almost scripted. Through my walk, I've discovered that you can speak to God just like a "Buddy"—not formal and rigid. The stories documented in *Unmasking Myths* have reinforced my personal thoughts on prayer. It doesn't have to be "religious" or scripted; we don't have to feel silly asking for the day-to-day things or wait to pray for the BIG things. God cares about it all! *Unmasking Myths* showed me there are others that are "on the same page" as me.
An inspiring read! Great for new Christians as well as long time believers.
– Elton Winkel

***

Hebrews 11:1
"Now faith is the substance of
things hoped for, the evidence
of things not seen."
Blessings &
M.A.Ward

Unmasking Myths

Is This Prayer?

MaryAnn Ward

Copyright

MaryAnn Ward Copyright 2020
All rights reserved.

Cover photo by **Helen Gwilliam**

Publisher's Cataloging-in-Publication Data
Names: Ward, MaryAnn, author.
Title: Unmasking myths : is this prayer? / MaryAnn Ward
Description: Balgonie, SK : ReMade Ministries, 2020. | Summary: Reveals truths about prayer through the experiences of ordinary people of all ages from around the world. These inspiring testimonies and scriptural content encourage everyone to encounter intimacy with God and experience prayer more powerfully.
Identifiers: ISBN 9781777130015 (pbk.) | ISBN 9781777130022 (hard cover) | ISBN 97817771316094 (ebook) | ISBN 9781777130039 (audio)
Subjects: LCSH: Christian Life. | Spiritual life – Christianity. | Prayer Christianity. | BISAC: RELIGION /Christian Living / Prayer. | RELIGION / Christian Living / Spiritual Growth. | RELIGION / Prayer.
Classification: LCC BV220 W373 | DDC 248.32--dc23

Published by ReMade Ministries
Box 205, Balgonie, SK S0G 0E0
Printed in Canada

Acknowledgments

When I sensed God encourage me to write a book on prayer, I gazed at my own library containing multiple volumes written by extraordinary men and women of prayer. Intimidation and inadequacy held me back for several months. I knew I was incapable of mastering such a project. God knew it too.

From the prayer room came a prompt to seek the help of a multitude of others, interviewing them about their personal prayer journeys. It is not hyperbole to say that the process has transformed my prayer life.

Unmasking Myths contains the wisdom of dozens of prayer warriors and intercessors of all ages and many nationalities. From Mongolia to Chile, nine to ninety years of age, housewives to doctors, they have given their personal perspectives on prayer. Their insights encourage us to pursue God through intimate relationship.

Their united voices speak through the pages of *Unmasking Myths,* declaring that prayer changes things—often circumstances and always us. I gratefully acknowledge the tremendous honor to tell their stories and share the wisdom they have gained on their knees in prayer.

They have shared with one intention only, that God would be glorified. A far second, but a desire nonetheless, is that the body of Christ would be built up, empowered and encouraged to **"pray without ceasing"** (1 Thess 5:17).

> **"Then Jesus told his disciples a parable**
> **to show them that they should always pray**
> **and not give up."**
> **Luke 18:1**

Thanks to each and every one of you. We are indebted to you.

v

Table of Contents

Introduction

Unmasking Myths developed a life of its own through countless interviews with people from multiple nations. The often raw, always real, experiences of ordinary Christians have had an undeniable impact on my life in gathering and gleaning from their stories. Their testimonies create a launch pad for increased prayer momentum across generations and denominations.

Even as they spoke of prayer, few realized how deeply their words were penetrating my heart—igniting hope and activating faith. Their combined experiences contain dozens of miraculous encounters, hundreds of years of wisdom, and thousands of hours of active prayer "duty" at the feet of Jesus.

As you read, you too will be challenged to encounter God in new ways, and enabled to see the fruit of vibrant prayer. Whether or not prayer is presently an active part of your daily routine, or you have enough knowledge to write a book on the topic yourself, *Unmasking Myths* will enhance anyone's prayer journey.

Hear the voices of those who have unmasked myths and discovered the power of prayer.

> *"Who can define prayer? It is a mystery. It is communion with God but more. It is the Lord doing what He does through human beings." – Sharon*

> *"You can talk to God every day—little things, big things, major things, small things. It doesn't matter. He cares about everything in your life." – Betty*

> *"Prayer is a continual dialogue we have with God, not in polished language but speaking what we feel." – Keegan*

CHAPTER 1
Brave Beginnings – Small Steps

> *"All along, prayer has been the Holy Spirit planting love in me for Jesus, coaxing it out."* – Meg

"Charlene, you have to pray!" Michelle's desperate tone on the video call took Charlene off guard.

"Right now? For what?" Charlene asked, as she noticed a woman sitting next to her friend.

As a massage therapist, Charlene's genuine concern for the welfare of others has helped her build strong relationships of trust among her clientele. Many of her clients, like Michelle, have become close friends.

Michelle's frantic words ran together like a messy collision between emergency and anticipation. "Charlene, you have to pray!" she pleaded, once again.

On her phone screen, Charlene saw that the woman sitting next to her friend was clearly distraught. Michelle quickly introduced her neighbor, who was seeking freedom from addictions and release from a traumatic past.

Though young in the faith, Charlene carries a boldness in prayer—prayer incubated in daily worship and sacred solitude with Jesus.

Though she felt unsure of the words to pray, Charlene slipped easily into interceding for the needs of a stranger. However, every sentence aimed toward Heaven was interrupted by Michelle. Charlene wondered whether either God or the two women on the other end of the video call understood anything she prayed.

"*Now*, Charlene!" Michelle interrupted yet again, '*The sinner's prayer*. Do it now!"

Surprised, Charlene asked Michelle's friend if she desired to commit her life to Christ.

"Yes, please!" she confirmed.

Charlene joyfully led another person to Jesus.

An alien became a citizen.

A lost child found her way home.

A woman bound by addiction was set free.

An aimless wanderer found

purpose and destiny.

With the past erased, a future unlocked and joy flooding away despair, the angels once again rejoiced (Lk 15:10). Thanks to the prayerful support of two ordinary women, an extraordinary relationship with Jesus Christ began. Perhaps the angels also shared a little head-scratching confusion and hand-slapping congratulations over humanity's blundering. Nonetheless, another sinner turned saint safely landed in the lap of their waiting Father.

"What is mankind that you are mindful of them,
human beings that you care for them?"
Psalm 8:4

Is this prayer? Does unorganized, frantic and incoherent prayer qualify? Yes, it certainly does.

What matters most in prayer is the sincerity of heart. Often, what makes no sense to our intellect makes perfect sense from God's perspective.

God responds to our plea in any language, under every

circumstance, from genuine seekers. He answers eloquent, well-planned, neatly scrolled prayers. He also responds to hurried, harried, broken prayer.

And yes, because of it, Heaven rejoices. I can think of no greater miracle than the transformation God does when someone yields their life to Him and

light invades darkness,

prison doors swing open,

sight fills once spiritually blind eyes,

and songs break forth from the

soil of despair.

> *"The more the person praying believes, the more catalytic how prayer will be fulfilled." – Patrick*

Personal Perspectives

As young as seven years old, Kevin wondered if God was real. Even though he went to church and took communion, Kevin felt there was an enormous distance between God and himself. As a young boy, whenever he had trouble falling asleep, he would reflect on God. Yet, he felt confused.

By the time he turned sixteen, the confusion had turned to fear. Though he assumed he was a Christian, he honestly didn't know what that meant. Only three years later, he was quickly heading in the wrong direction.

"Back home from my first year of university, I was working for the town. However, because of a severe spinal injury from playing hockey, I couldn't do anything without being loaded up on prescription painkillers. When I came to the end of summer, I had no money left. I was drinking daily and spending every

3

penny at the local bar. I was on a destructive track.

"Here I was, a nineteen-year-old guy who couldn't even stand up straight or sit down. Depressed, I didn't want to go back to university the way I was. Everything was on a bad track, although I maybe wasn't aware of it. My family had been set free from alcoholism. However, I was on a personal journey of recovery from being raised in a dysfunctional home.

"I met Merodee and beyond question fell in love with her at first sight. She and her sister were crossing the street right in front of my vehicle. I slammed on the brakes to avoid hitting them. We held eye contact as she passed by.

"Shortly afterward, I invited her to a football game. Merodee brought some Christian music with her, and saying nothing she took my music out of the cassette player and put hers in. We listened to her music on the way to the football game and back again. All I listened to for the next couple of days were the tapes she had left in my car. I was so enamored by Merodee that her music captivated me.

"A little while later, I drove out to an old country church and parked outside the locked gate. I sat there, a nervous wreck, feeling very emotional.

"Suddenly, the palpable Presence of God entered my car."

"I started to talk to God, and He started to answer me. I knew, with no one ever telling me, what to do to be in a relationship with Him. I confessed my sins and asked Him into my life. It was such an incredibly emotional experience I couldn't even drive. I probably sat there for half an hour, unable to leave.

"I didn't understand anything, except I knew it was God. I knew God wanted a relationship with me.

"When I cried out, He was immediately present, closer than

anything I had ever felt. I don't know if I had any other impression except knowing what I needed was God.

"That was the beginning of prayer for me when I felt the Presence of God for the first time. Looking back, I can close my eyes and still see everything and feel the same feeling, though not with the same emotion. Before then, I didn't even know if I believed in God. Yet, He revealed Himself to me in an unforgettable way.

"Afterward, I phoned Merodee and told her what had happened. She yelled into the phone, 'You're saved!'

" 'What does that mean?' I had asked. I didn't even know.

"I'm a little naïve as to what the Lord delivered me from. I can't imagine where the track I was on would have led if I hadn't encountered God in that season."

Mark said,

"Letting go of the idea that I can somehow earn or merit God's love has perhaps been the greatest obstacle to resting in Him and enjoying His Presence, where legitimate prayer begins."

Yoge began her relationship with Jesus while living in her home country of India.

"When I was young, my grandmother was experiencing many problems. Someone invited her to church and told her about Jesus. They said, 'If you pray there, everything will be all right.'

"As a result, my grandmother was the first one in our family

5

to accept Jesus and become a secret worshiper of God. When I was about four years old, she started taking me to church too, but I didn't realize what was going on. Maybe God chose me then, but it took many years for me to come to Him.

"In India, our work also determines our religion and cast. My private math tutor belonged to our cast. He was the one who helped me realize who Jesus was. If he wouldn't have been from our cast, I wouldn't have listened to him when he said, 'You need to know you aren't worshiping a real God, but worshiping idols instead. You shouldn't do that.'

"I thought, 'I know you. Why are you saying our god is not a god?' I asked, 'What happened to you? What made you convert to Christianity?'

"He said, 'No, it's true! We are all idol worshipers.'

" 'Okay, let it be an idol.' I said, 'We're living a sophisticated life, doing what we want to do. Compared to other people, our standard of living is very good. What is there to blame this god for?'

"He said, 'It isn't the idol giving this to you; it is your living Father who is providing for you.'

" 'How can you prove it?'

"He continued, 'What if you have a kitty and think your pet is a god? One day the pet dies. You cry because you aren't ready to believe your pet is dead. You say to the dead kitty, 'I feel hungry and don't know what to do.' You're asking something dead to give you food. Will the dead pet give you food? Or will your mother, who is listening to you cry, give you food? Who will give you food?'

" 'Obviously, my mother,' I said, 'the dead pet can't give me food.'

" 'Yes!' he said, 'The living God is the One who provides all these things you're asking for. Still, you believe your dead kitty is giving you food. It is not the dead kitty but your living mother who feeds you. In the same way, when you are worshiping and praying to an idol, your living Father God in Heaven listens to you and provides you with all the good things you ask for. It is the living God, not dead idols, who gives you all these things. Your Father in Heaven is watching you, knowing what His daughter needs, but sees she doesn't know who to ask.'

"While he was talking to me, he was weeping bitterly. He spoke a simple word, but it was completely anointed. His weeping touched me deeply as I carefully listened to his words. God gave me the understanding that I had been praying to an idol, while He, my living Father, was beside me providing whatever I asked for.

"As I walked home, those thoughts rewound in my mind. I closed my eyes and started crying as I realized what I was doing when I worshiped our god. I knew what I was doing wasn't good. I asked forgiveness from my living Father in Heaven. 'I'm not going to worship idols anymore.' I said, 'I am going to live my entire life for You.'

"I started going to church every Sunday, but soon my dad discovered I was worshiping Jesus. One day when I came home from church, he was ready to throw a brick at me to kill me. Because we were religious leaders in our cast, he said, 'I will kill you. I won't allow you to live as a Christian.' He also threatened to pour kerosene on me and burn me. The second time, he poured it on my head, but my grandmother came and saved me. Before going to church each Sunday, I mentally prepared myself for the beating I would get when I returned home.

"From the day I became a worshiper of Jesus Christ, I was crazy about God. I felt like He was sitting right beside me, talking to me. People wondered what happened and told me to limit my worship and devotion to God, but I never wanted to.

"I couldn't believe it! All this time I had worshiped lifeless idols. When I came to God, I knew, beyond a doubt, He was alive, sitting with me and talking to me. I felt Him moving all around me. Whatever I asked for in prayer happened. How do you deny it? No one can deny it!

"That's how my journey with Jesus Christ began."

For Shelly, prayer was a natural overflow of the relationship she entered with God. She tells her story,

"I had made many poor decisions that eventually landed me into an abusive relationship with someone who completely isolated me. I had never felt so much hatred and was devastated. I didn't know there could be so much darkness. I would wake up thinking I was in a nightmare, but it was real. To him, it was a big game; he was grossly unfaithful. It was like I was trying to get out of my skin and away from the pain, but I couldn't get free.

"In desperation, I made an appointment to go through the steps of freedom through a ministry called Freedom in Christ. During those sessions, I received Jesus Christ as my Savior and began a personal relationship with Him.

"After two sessions lasting nine hours (spending most of the time on forgiveness), I forgave him and everyone else in my life. It was like everything dropped off me. In its place, I could feel God's love being poured inside me.

"As God's incredible love overwhelmed me, I instinctively knew that a relationship with Jesus Christ was where I wanted and needed to be forever. Looking back, I remembered experiencing the same love when I was four years old.

"I walked away totally changed—no longer consumed by hatred

but overwhelmed by God's love. I had all kinds of grace for this man, tried to help him and prayed for him. But I got out."

As a child, Rachel moved to Canada where she became a Christian.

"I was born in China and lived there for eight years before coming to Canada. We didn't hear about the name of Jesus or Christianity in China. There were posters about evolution everywhere. I was afraid that one day I would turn into a monkey in a cage instead of a human being.

"In China, school is very competitive, but you're supposed to be friends with everyone in your classroom. One week before we left China, I had an argument with a classmate over an origami crane I had made. She found my crane and turned it into a frog. When I discovered my crane had disappeared, I became angry. Normally, I wouldn't start a quarrel, but this time I did.

"In China, if a dispute arose, a class monitor would come to the class to help settle the problem. The girl told the monitor I had lost my crane out of irresponsibility, so when she found it she made it into a frog. She kept crying and won the sympathy of the class monitor. They forced me to leave school permanently because of the argument.

" 'Okay, I will leave,' I had thought, 'but where will I go?'

"God used this incident to prepare me to move away. Right after the dispute, I discovered my dad and I were soon leaving to live in Canada. My grandmother, the first Christian in our family, had been praying for us to receive Christ.

"God, by His sovereign will works through people in unusual ways. We had a friend from China who enrolled at

Trinity Western University because a consultant who did not know Jesus specifically told her to go to this Christian University. It was there that her favorite memories developed and she first learned about Jesus. Even though we don't always understand how God moves, whether through arguments, class monitors or unbelieving consultants, God is working in our lives.

"As a child, I would believe whatever my dad told me. When I was little, he told me Buddha held the earth. We didn't know about Jesus then, but when we came to Canada, Dad became a Christian. Dad told me about Jesus and why He had to die for our sins. Until then, I had thought Jesus was a rebel. When God spoke to me through my dad, I considered becoming a Christian. I didn't ask Jesus into my heart yet, though.

"My first impression of Jesus was that He was like Santa. You could ask Him for something and He would give it to you. Later, I found out He is bigger than that. He is God and works the big picture. He desires for us all to come to Him, so He can give us His grace.

"I started to change when I was nine years old and Jesus became personal. I prayed, but at first, my prayers were self-centered. Then I realized my parents also had needs. I started to pray for people to be healed and began to understand Jesus' love for others."

No matter what age, stage or circumstance of life, the prayer of committing one's life to the Lordship of Jesus Christ is the most powerful, miracle-working prayer anyone could pray.

Unmasking the Myth

One myth has kept many people from committing their lives to Jesus Christ and finding the love Shelly spoke about. This myth declares any god will do.

> *"We can always have a non-god to go to instead of God."*
> *– Karin*

Only Jesus can create the profound change Charlotte, Kevin and millions of others have experienced. Jesus desires for everyone to come to know the one and only true God.

> **"Now this is eternal life: that they know you,**
> **the *only* true God, and Jesus Christ, whom**
> **you have sent."**
> **John 17:3**
> **(Emphasis mine)**

This same intimate relationship with God these people have spoken about is available right now to any who will sincerely come to Him.

> **"He longs for everyone to embrace his life**
> **and return to the full knowledge of the truth."**
> **1 Timothy 2:4 TPT**

God is waiting for everyone to embrace Him and the life He offers. God loves us and has an incredible plan for our future, regardless of our past (Ps 139:16). He desires for us to have a fulfilling, exciting life right now and forever—a life connected with Him (Jn 10:10).

Kate asked,

"Does any other god communicate back to you? Does any other god respond to you like the Lord God? Does any other god give you life? Can another god forgive your sins?

"Jesus Christ is life. He gives us an unbelievable life now. Eternal life! Life is found in Jesus Christ alone. In Him is everything I need to exist—love, joy, peace and so much more. I don't want to look anywhere else or to anything else. Time is too precious to waste pursuing other so-called gods.

"God is a life-giving Spirit. When You know your spirit is made alive by God's Spirit, that's it! You need nothing else.

"The ultimate, Almighty God, is available. He is the One living, true God. Until you meet Jesus, you don't know what you are missing."

> *"To communicate with Almighty God is incredible. Knowing He wants to have fellowship with us is very humbling. It is the ultimate relationship to have."*

Only one thing keeps us from experiencing this vital relationship with Him. God is holy and perfect. Only those who are without sin can come into His Presence and enjoy His wonderful plan and experience His Presence. Every one of us has sinned and comes far short of God's perfect standard (Rom 3:23).

God provided the solution for restoring intimacy with us through Jesus Christ, His Son. Jesus died on the cross to take our punishment and pay the price for our sins (Rom 5:8). It didn't end there! On the third day, Jesus rose from the grave as the giver of life for all (Rom 6:23).

The Bible says that by repenting and confessing the Lordship of Jesus, we can then live in a relationship with God. It sounds too simple for such a complicated problem (Rom 10:9-10). However, by accepting God's provision and committing our lives to Him, He makes everything new.

Like a baby begins to walk by taking tiny steps, we begin the fascinating journey of faith through a seemingly small prayer spoken from sincere hearts. If you want to take this life-changing step today, Jesus is only a prayer away.

> *"The root of every prayer journey is a relationship with Jesus." — Jan*

> *"Dear God, I confess I have sinned against You and others. I choose today to believe Jesus died on the cross for the forgiveness of my sins. I turn from the way I have been living to follow You. Please forgive me and come into my life. I trust in You and desire for You to be my Lord and Savior from this day forward, in Jesus' Name (Rom 10:13, Jn 20:31). Thank You, Lord, for all You have done for me. Thank You for Your love and the gift of Your saving grace."*

> *"God wants to know me and make Himself known to me." — Heather*

***

> *"Prayer comes out of a place of being fully known. It is an evolving journey out of our relationship with the Lord." — Kristina*

***

> *"Prayer is a grace gift." — Merodee*

CHAPTER 2

Create Connection – Build Relationship

> *"It is the little things I look forward to in prayer, like saying, 'Holy Spirit, what are You working on this week?' and then leaving it open. That is a part of the living conversation."*
> — *Lowell*

A decade of depression, suicidal thoughts and addictions merged the hopelessness of youth with the reality of adulthood. There she stood on the precipice of despondency, fully prepared to step into the finality of death.

Through the icy stillness of the winter night, she stumbled. The crunch of frigid snow beneath her feet uttered the only sound, breaking the barren silence. Her breaths froze, suspended in wispy strands.

As she collapsed in a snowbank, a revelation of the Father's love broke through the stony crust of her own heart. Flashbacks of traumatic life moments rolled through her mind like an unwanted movie, but tonight she saw God's protective hand overshadowing her in each of the scenes. Suddenly, memories were no longer cloaked with shame, regret or pain, but with an unshakeable knowing of God's abiding Presence.

Kneeling in the snow, she whispered past freezing tears, "God, I have nothing to offer You but broken fragments. If You want me, I am Yours."

Is this prayer when words
    hang frail and lifeless,
        are scant in knowledge but
            stretch long in meaning,
                ebb from the brokenness of soul and
                    whisper to unseen ear?

> *"The simplest prayers of a new Christian have the greatest faith." — Clay*

For the first time in months, she cast her gaze upward. Aurora borealis danced in rhythmic freedom to unheard melodies. The stars appeared more brilliant than she ever remembered. Something within her once dead now vibrated with inexpressible life. A relationship she always craved, but never knew existed, was birthed in a moment.

She turned away
    from death's evil intent,
        toward love's embrace,
            against boundless hope,
                beneath the wings of courage,
                  along the path of life.

For her, a Bible was unattainable, church unreachable and Christian fellowship unheard of. Simple, genuine and often raw prayer became the umbilical cord of sustaining strength.

A toddler's time on her knees forms co-ordination patterns instrumental to learn how to walk and run. Similarly, humble prayer gives a magnificent perspective for Christians, foundational to all other spiritual development and growth.

Like a little child, she soon recognized the voice of her Father. Her ears tuned naturally to hear Him as she waited and listened.

Though she had no biblical reference point for it, the conception of dreams and visions formed her fledgling belief system.

> **"And afterward; I will pour out my spirit on all**
> **people. Your sons and daughters will prophesy,**
> **your old men will dream dreams, your**
> **young men will see visions."**
> **Joel 2:28**

Not long after her conversion, she awoke from sleep by a blinding light—light brighter than any natural light. It intensified as it drew near. Fear and awe snatched her breath away. The Light stopped at the foot of her bed. She recognized Him immediately as she whispered His name almost imperceptibly, "Jesus."

In His eyes she saw the life she craved,
a love overflowing with passion and void of shame,
a joy free and abandoned,
a peace transcending anything hoped for,
and unlimited power moving within
Him, through Him, and around Him, filling every molecule in the room. Her body vibrated in His Presence.

With Him was complete acceptance. Hope to believe and strength to endure awakened within her, as if by the dawning of a fresh day. That one encounter would be enough to carry her through the solitary season ahead.

God continued to speak, and she continued to listen. He spoke in the breeze of the country wind. She could feel His Presence in the flowers, trees and steep banks of the valleys and hills. He taught her lessons through ranching and gardening, marriage and parenting, friendships and community.

> **"For since the creation of the world God's invisible**
> **qualities —his eternal power and divine nature—**
> **have been clearly seen, being understood from**
> **what has been made, so that people are**
> **without excuse."**
> **Romans 1:20**

God's voice though not audible was distinct; without words, she began to discover His character and His ways.

> *"The more I learn to talk with Jesus,*
> *the more I learn about the Father in Heaven."*
> *— Karli*

Over a year after her relationship with Jesus Christ began, she received the most welcome of gifts—a Bible. Her famished soul refused to be satisfied as hour after fleeting hour she read and studied its pages. Now she heard His voice embedded in each word and line. His words were

rich and powerful,
strong and sure,
tender and firm,
instructive and encouraging,
milk and meat,
fulfilling and sustaining.

She had questions; He held the answers. He would speak; she would listen and ponder. The language of childhood prayer was giving way to the adolescence of increased understanding. Faith rose on the waves of quiet trust, ebbing and flowing with comfort and ease. The solid foundation of prayer, based not on denomination or tradition, but Holy Spirit lessons, proved solid.

Prayer is living communication with God, ever-changing and deepening. It begins with a limited vocabulary, poor pronunciation, no sentence structure, and selfish focus, but with maturity, articulation improves.

> *"Prayer is a journey beginning with a personal*
> *relationship and never really ends." — Mark*

Personal Perspectives

We experience many types of relationships in life: parent and child; husband and wife; student and teacher; friend to friend. As a single mother, Shelly came to know God intimately as her Husband and Father.

"Every day for probably three years, I would read Isaiah 54 and pray to God as my husband, 'The Lord will be my Husband. The Lord of Heaven's Armies is His Name. He is my Redeemer.'

"I would often think of Boaz and Ruth in comparison to the husband-wife relationship God had with me. **'Though the mountains be shaken and the hills be removed, yet my unfailing love for you will not be shaken . . . All your children will be taught by the LORD, and great will be their peace'** (Is 54:10,13).

"At least once a day in my quiet time with God, I would pray these verses talking to God as my Husband. During this time I went to a prophetic conference, sitting about halfway back. The prophet walked around prophesying over people. He came and prophesied over me. Then he went over to someone else, but soon he came back and stopped beside me. Again and again, he went away and came back, stopping beside me each time.

" 'Why do I get something every time I go past you?' he asked.

"I laughed to myself thinking, 'Because I am His wife. You have God's wife in the room.' It was neat how the relationship I had with God was expressed so tangibly.

"Anytime something is going on with my kids, I pray, 'Lord, You told me . . . I am trusting You. I believe You. If they are going to experience great peace, You are their Father. I'm giving this back to You because You are the Head of our house.'

"Having God as my Husband and knowing Him as Father answered so many questions and concerns for me. As a young single mother, it was a great relief. I have never had specific verses I've dwelt on every day like I did those during that season.

"I thought, 'I can't prosper because I'm a single mom and I can't be a giver.' Then I heard Him say, 'You can be prosperous and you can be hugely generous because I am your Husband and your Provider.'

"The reality of that relationship was transformational."

Kimberly remarked,

"Prayer is as intimate and close as if I'm talking to my closest friend. On one hand, it's like sitting down having coffee with a friend, but there is a holiness, reverence and fear you experience because prayer is such a privilege. You are interacting with the Creator of the universe who wants to have a relationship with you."

Emmanuel is also gaining insight into his relationship and intimacy with God.

"Since the beginning, God created us for intimacy. Destiny and purpose are different. Adam and Eve were destined to be fruitful and multiply, but their purpose was an intimate relationship with God. So often we put things to do *for* the Lord ahead of being *with* Him.

"God tells us to **'Trust in the Lord with all (our) heart and lean not on (our) own understanding; in all (our) ways submit to him, and he will make (our) paths straight'** (Prv 3:5-6).

"The word 'acknowledge' or 'submit' is the same as 'intimacy.' In all your ways know Him, and He will direct your paths. He is asking me to be with Him. I don't need to understand everything, but I just trust He is directing me.

"It is out of this relationship that He asks us to partner with Him. We have authority with the Father in sonship.

"Proverbs 25:2 reminds us **'It is the glory of God to conceal a matter; to search out a matter is the glory of kings.'** There are things to be discovered in prayer. They are not hidden from us but are for us to search out. God is interested in the journey and He wants us to get there with Him.

> *"God doesn't hide from us but for us to find Him. Hide and seek only gets exciting when we find the one we are looking for."*

Everyone's journey is unique, but often not without struggle. Jennifer shares her experience,

"When I was a kid, although we had the habit of praying, we didn't have a personal relationship with Jesus. My view of God was a guy with white hair in the clouds ready to throw lightning bolts. I feared Him. If I did something wrong, He would punish me. I knew my family loved me, but I didn't know God loved me. My belief in God was reward and punishment based, so my understanding of a relationship with God was harsh.

"Until I was eleven years old, there was a disconnect. Then my parents both accepted Jesus as their Savior.

"I saw my dad go from severely depressed, suicidal and angry to being kind. When Dad started praying, there was such a change in his demeanor that even financial pressure didn't shake him. When the bank came and took the machinery, Dad was totally in control of his emotions as he sat at the kitchen table praying.

"I saw prayer wasn't just a bedtime thing, but something you could do any time. There was something about the way Dad conducted our family after that, which spoke volumes to me. He started praying for all of us to come to know the Lord in a personal relationship.

> *"Prayer changed for me when I saw how prayer changed my Dad."*

"Instead of being needs-based, prayer became simpler and more personal.

"After Dad died, I was angry with God and didn't feel I could trust Him. I did a lot of yelling both internally and externally and was miserable to be around. Through Dad's death, the seed of doubt grew and clouded everything I thought about God. 'Should I pray? Why should I pray?' When I was angry with God, I thought of Him as a genie in a bottle.

"My prayer journey is better now because I'm seeing it as a relationship again. Instead of trying to say the right thing and do the right thing, I can ask Him for strength to accept what He has for me and receive His help to do whatever He wants. My prayers aren't 'do it my way' anymore.

"I know even if I fail ten times out of ten, I can recognize my weakness and bask in His strength."

For Joy, discovering Jesus and coming into a relationship with Him, developed later in life.

"My brother was into New Age and had given me books to read about it. One booklet talked about a woman who had gone to Heaven and came back down. I don't know why, but I took the little booklet to my Mennonite neighbor who I knew was kind and loving.

"She was wise, read the book and called me a week later. Then she shared with me the Five Spiritual Laws explaining how to have a relationship with Jesus and gave me a modern translation of the Bible. I knew about Jesus, but no one had ever told me about a personal relationship with Him before.

"While reading the Bible a light seemed to go on when I read **'by grace you have been saved, through faith'** (Eph 2:8). I called my neighbor and told her I believe. She invited me to a Christian women's club which taught about salvation. Once when one speaker was standing by herself, I approached her. It registered in my heart and mind when she read the sinner's prayer with me.

"I immediately lost all interest in reading any of my brother's books. It was settled in my heart; God did something in me.

"It's the little things that make it personal. Our relationship isn't about putting Him on and taking Him off before and after church. In a relationship, you want to be connected all the time. Our relationship with God is knowing He is with us every moment of the day. That's exciting for me and gets better all the time."

I appreciated Aimee's transparency as she told me her story.

"In my childhood, I probably thought of God as a Papa figure. I felt like I was there leaning on His chest, listening to His voice and had a sense He was talking to me too. I don't know how I knew, but I have always had an awareness of God.

"From early childhood into my preteen years, I don't remember praying for myself much. I relied on my parent's faith, so prayer wasn't personal then. Then from preteen into high school, prayer was something for tough situations like, 'Help me pass this exam or do this assignment.'

"About two years ago at a youth retreat, I had an encounter with God. The Papa relationship came back. I was at the altar during one of the evening services, rocked by the worship and felt the Presence of God. Pastor Rob came and prayed in tongues[1] over me. I heard God say, 'Aimee, will you give me your "Yes?"' ' I responded immediately, 'Yes, Papa.'

"I became intrigued by God and more serious about my relationship with Him. I started Master's Commission, a discipleship training program, in Grade 12. Then I moved to the city and became involved in a community group. My prayer life is more constant now. Before I thought God was distant, but now I know He is right beside me, listening to me.

"It has taken me a long time to get to the place where I can say to God, 'Here is my heart.' Even though I knew He knows everything, I was always afraid to say it myself.

"God will not force intimacy."

"Intimacy is a choice. Every prayer counts because prayer is rooted in intimacy with God. I'm finding as I grow in intimacy my faith for answers grows, and an ability to know what to pray for."

Most people spoke of relational intimacy as a natural component of their faith. Staci gave a humorous illustration I won't soon forget.

"Several times, we have had conversations with our kids about what to do when our relationship with God isn't easy. One thing we have told them is just to keep talking to Him and keep going to the Word of God. At the same time, I have wrestled with that kind of consistency myself.

"A friend reminded me we don't need to worry about getting too proud or distant. We know God could always send a whale to keep us on track, just like He did for Jonah (Jon 2:10). I find that oddly reassuring. Even though I don't want to be whale barf, I trust God cares about this relationship more than I can imagine. He will bring me back to Himself.

"We don't take advantage of His grace, but we know He will do whatever is necessary to keep our relationship where He wants it to be."

Jesus said to His disciples,

"I no longer call you servants, because a servant does not know his master's business. Instead, I have called you friends, for everything that I learned from my Father I have made known to you."
John 15:15

Miranda is short on years, but long in maturity. She values her relationship with God both as Father and Friend. She says,

"Sometimes, I find it easier to talk to Dad about certain things than anyone else. It is special when God is our Father, and we are His children. We can come to God, talking with Him about anything and trusting Him whether it is about a good or bad situation. I can apologize for things I have done, ask for help in situations or tell Him how I'm feeling.

"I know I'm talking to God and He is listening and talking to me too. When He speaks it always lines up with what the Bible says.

"I pray way more now than I did before. It is easy talking to God when you know He is your best Friend."

Patrick shares about the shift from seeing himself as a servant to knowing he is a son of the Father.

"If you are praying as a servant, you are pleading for something. Then there will always be questions, 'Have I served You right today to ask this of You? Did I do enough today to earn Your favor?' When I am approaching the Lord as His servant, I am asking if it is His will. As a servant, there is always a reason in my mind that it will not be God's will.

"When I come to God as a son, there is nothing I can do to make it not His will. I may not be mature enough for Him to hand me the keys for the big thing I'm praying for, but as a son, His grace compels me into that level of maturity."

So, who is this God who invites us into relationship? Is He
our best Friend,
our beautiful, kind Lover,
our ferocious King,
our gentle Father,
or our Counsellor?
Which one is He, or is He all of these and more? Is this prayer if we approach God in such varying ways?

For most people I talked with, their relationship with God morphed and matured through the years. The more they grew in understanding His love, the consistency of His character and His faithful commitment to a relationship with them, the deeper the intimate trust developed.

> "I always knew prayer was talking to God, but now
> I'm discovering prayer is hearing God too.
> It goes two ways." — Pearl

Few people spoke of this relationship in depth. Yet, they all experienced the depth of relationship woven together inseparably in mutual love and satisfaction. Such a relationship goes beyond human understanding. Prayer, the two-way communication of speaking and listening, is strategic in developing this bond.

Isaac agrees,

"There is a misconception about prayer. It isn't sending up a need, *hoping* God answers. Rather, it is a two-way conversation. Instead of throwing prayers up and moving on, I've learned how to have a praying lifestyle.

"When I read Colossians 4:2 about continuing in prayer and watching with thanksgiving, it changed my prayer life. My relationship with God suddenly became real to me. That relationship changes everything! I knew I couldn't just pray and walk away doing my own thing like before.

> "God has shown me I can't do anything
> outside of His love."

"Through relationship, I come to know who God is and live my life with a dependency on Him. I honestly don't want anything in my life to be without Him. He is loving enough to tell me how much I need Him. When I know who He is, I can ask according to His character. Jesus said, '. . . **apart from me you can do nothing'** (Jn 15:5). Apart from my relationship with Him, there is nothing! It all comes from talking to Him and being still enough to listen."

I'll let Staci have the last word.

"Often, our understanding of prayer is one directional rather than conversational. It is about talking more than listening. That's why we don't feel like we hear from God or our prayer isn't doing much.

"In our Bible study group, we pray and listen to what God wants to speak to each other. Prayer is living. Anytime the Holy Spirit speaks to us, it is a part of the conversation with God. Then we have to respond to His voice one way or another. Our response is still a part of that conversation.

"Lowell and I have been married for almost twenty three years now. We specifically set aside our Friday nights as our date night. We look forward to our time together and enjoy it. It is an important part of our relationship.

"With our family, we do life together. Those conversations happen, but much more so because Holy Spirit inhabits us and is always with us. Even though our kids are fifteen and seventeen now, we still come together to pray as a family before they go to bed. It is during these intentional times when big conversations come up. These are specific times we set aside where we group, talk and have community time together.

"That's what it is like with God. Our devotion time is set aside time to come together, like our date night or prayer time with the kids. Prayer time is a specific community time with God. During the rest of our life, there is still the element of ongoing togetherness with God and Holy Spirit.

"My growth in my relationship with God is connected with that ongoing conversation with Him—at least as much as making sure I carve out quiet time alone with Him. When I listen, I cultivate the idea of, 'Holy Spirit, what do you want?' "

Unmasking the Myth

Many people believe God exists. However, many also believe the myth that God has abandoned humanity to survive alone and figure things out for themselves.

Understanding that the God of all gods and Lord of all lords invites and welcomes us into a relationship is difficult to fathom. Neither lack of faith nor understanding alters the truth. God pursues a relationship with each person far more than we could ever comprehend.

Prayer is rooted in our relationship with the person of Jesus Christ. Every opportunity to speak to Him and to recognize His responses to us is nothing short of miraculous.

Jesus paved the way for us through the cross.

> **"Let us then approach God's throne of grace with confidence, so that we may receive mercy and find grace to help us in our time of need."**
> **Hebrews 4:16**

Keegan explains,

"There are a lot of different world views. For Christians, it is humbling and awe-inspiring to know we have a personal relationship with Jesus Christ. It is inclusive in the sense that anyone can come to the Father. At the same time, it is exclusive in that Jesus is the only way to Him.

"Because of what Christ did at the cross, through His death and resurrection, we all can converse with Him without a liaison.

> *"The Creator of the universe who put everything into motion takes time to answer my prayers and show interest in my life."*

"That relational access sets Christianity apart from every other religion."

Though a relationship with Jesus Christ is available, it is up to each one of us to welcome Him into our lives and begin to exercise that privilege. The Bible is the primary way God speaks to us. Conversational prayer is the primary way we speak to Him.

Prayer flows naturally and uncomplicated out of our relationship with God. Even the youngest child can pray. The first prayer might be,

> *"God, I want to know You. Help me to be sensitive to Your Presence and voice. I desire a relationship with You as my Father, Friend, Counsellor, Source, and Lord."*

Then take a moment to listen.

If you don't have a Bible, there are many downloadable versions available. Begin reading in the Book of John or one of the other Gospels to start. As you read, listen for God to speak directly to you. His voice will usually come in the form of a thought, but one you know didn't originate within you.

Soon you will find Him nudging your spirit,
encouraging you with hope and confidence,
providing wisdom for your daily decisions,

revealing His love for you, and
showing His goodness in all situations.
God has not abandoned us to our undoing, but is only a whisper away.

"Prayer is an ongoing thing—speaking to Him and hearing from Him throughout the day. I never turn prayer off." – Karli

***

"Something extravagant happened at the cross. He sounds different, looks different and is approachable." – Perry

***

"Prayer is co-existence with Papa, Jesus, and Holy Spirit. It is communication that doesn't always need words." – Heather

***

Notes:
1. Dennis & Rita Bennett, *The Holy Spirit & You: A Guide to the Spirit-Filled Life* (Newberry, Bridge-Logos Publishers, 1971, 1998, 56.
(Dennis & Rita Bennett explain praying in tongues as, "Speaking in tongues is prayer with and in the Spirit—it is our spirit speaking to God, inspired by the Holy Spirit.")

CHAPTER 3

Sons & Daughters
– Childlike Faith

> *"The understanding that God rejoices over us—*
> *rejoicing over His sons and daughters—*
> *has kept me joyful and childlike."*
> *– Candice*

While grasping the weathered leather strap of the sliding barn door with both hands, Anne raised her left foot against the door frame. Using all her eight-year-old strength, she pulled with her arms while simultaneously pushing with her leg. The massive door refused to release its claw-like grip. Again and again, she yanked against the unmoving hulk.

"No!" she cried in frustration.

Her head fell in exhaustion, pressing against the slivered wood door. Hot tears of defeat ran down her flushed cheeks and splattered in the dust between her feet. Squaring her shoulders and pulling herself erect, she glared at the door with renewed determination.

Once again, Anne wrapped her small hands around the smooth,

hardened strap. Planting one foot on the ground and the other braced waist height on the door frame, she yanked and pushed. This time, she felt it ever so slightly give way. Resolve outmeasured Anne's stature by a country mile. Inch-by-inch, the door released its hold to form a gap barely large enough for her to wedge herself through. With a sense of triumph, she squeezed her way into the barn and eased the door shut to conceal her whereabouts.

It took a moment for her eyes to adjust to the soft light ebbing through the dusty panes of four small square windows set in the barn's exterior wall. Heading to the wooden ladder, Anne ascended to the loft, lifting and twisting the heavy wooden hatch to gain access to the upper level of the barn. Only when the hatch was firmly in place did she breathe deep.

Before the first break of dawn,

before the rooster's time-setting crow,

before her eyes had fully opened,

before the aroma of her father's morning coffee, here is where Anne wanted to be.

The smells and sounds within the old barn soothed and quieted the discord within her young heart. The sights here were familiar and loved. Here her soul found rest.

Unlike the lower level, the loft was bright. The large south-facing opening allowed the sun to warm and infuse every corner of Anne's "secret place" with light. A soft pile of loose hay welcomed her to come and lie down. The mingled fragrance of alfalfa and sweet clover wafted over her as thick layers of dust swayed peacefully in abandoned web hammocks far above her head. She watched golden dust fragments swirl in sparkling torrents upon beams of light.

The stillness here invited Anne to close her eyes and listen. At first, she heard only the continuous motion of swallow wings swooping up and then away from their nest high above the gaping hole.

Soon, Anne heard the unsung melody within her own heart. Then just as sure, she heard *Him* respond in perfect harmony—the gentle duet of common union. Hours felt like moments here. Even hunger was powerless to draw her away.

The solitude invited Anne to press beyond the natural rhythms of life. This secure loft

heard secrets and held tears,
gave room for both dreamer and dreams,
watched twirling dances of reckless abandon,
birthed courage to endure and faith to stand,
conceived a love deeper than imagination,
whispered peace to a wounded heart, and
sheltered her to rest while releasing her to run.

Is this prayer? The silent whispers of a child's heart?

Here in the loft, the power of, and undying need for, the Presence of God germinated in the tender soil of childhood. Here her faith took form and became tangible. God birthed, in humble seclusion, the habit of listening and speaking with bold simplicity. Though alone, Anne was never alone. In life-giving stillness, she was welcomed into relationship with the God she did not know—yet, who always knew her.

Through the decades, prayer grew increasingly palpable. It's a condition of a heart tenderly tuned to the whispers of God.

In the innocence of childhood,
through the uncertainty of youth,
the pressures of marriage and family,
and the labors of responsibility,
the habit of prayer solidified.

In often unseen places, encounters with God have been experienced by both the young and the young at heart.

> *"I had to choose to allow my heart to be more childlike."*
> *– Amanda* [F.]

Personal Perspectives

When Jan was only three years old, she was drawn to Jesus through a children's Bible book.

"When I saw pictures of Jesus in a children's book in the dentist's office, I immediately wanted to know Him. I don't know where my mother purchased a copy of the book, but I insisted she read it to me every night. I would know if she tried to hurry or miss a page. I wanted every word about Jesus.

"After she tucked me into bed, I would pray, 'Jesus, I want to see You and know You. I want to walk in the garden with You like in the book.'

"One night, Jesus came right into my room filling it with light. I felt His love. I was instantly in awe of His holiness, His God-ness. I pulled the blanket over my eyes. His holiness was overwhelming.

" 'No! I *want* to know Him and to see Him,' I thought.

"I pulled the blanket down and felt His hug, before watching Him leave through my window. From that moment on, to know Him, see Him, and be close to Him was sealed in my heart. No one could tell me He wasn't real.

> *"The root of every prayer journey is a relationship with Jesus."*

"My mom wouldn't take me to church, but my great-aunt started taking me when I was eight years old. In the prayer room of a downtown mission church, I recognized the same light, love, and Presence of God as when Jesus came into my room. The prayer room became my favorite place.

"Until then, being alone with Jesus was enough. I already knew Him as my best Friend and my God. The prayer room broadened my perspective.

"As I heard other people pray, I learned distinct parts of God's heart. I discovered He could use even a child like me to encourage and pray for others. While babies and children slept in the pews, women cried for hours praying for wayward sons and daughters. The voices of grown men thundered the Word of God through the room with authority and faith. Even as a child, I understood the unique expressions of prayer and knew God received it all. I sensed this was a good and safe place."

Hearing God at such a young an age is not uncommon. Little hearts are finely tuned to the frequency of His voice. Children can be drawn into a relationship with Him and more. Candice shares her experience as a child.

"When I was three years old, I would wake up each morning hearing my dad praying in the living room. More than saying the words, he would sing in a language I didn't know. His prayers didn't sound desperate, but more like an invitation.

"One morning, I felt the Presence of the Lord so tangibly I wanted to walk with my dad. The Presence of the Holy Spirit captivated me. I wanted to be where God's Presence was, so I crawled out of my bed to be with my dad.. Without hesitation, he took my little hand in his, allowing me to join him as he continued to walk, sing and pray.

"Because my parents were assistant pastors, we would go to church twice a day. Soon after experiencing the Presence of God with my dad, I asked my mom if I could go to pre-service prayer. She said, 'Yes,' but reminded me not to fool around.

"I knelt beside a chair and started praying in tongues. Mom didn't know it at first, but leaned close and realized I was being filled with the Holy Spirit.

"Before long, it was time for the service. Mom didn't want me to draw attention to myself, but I was still praying in tongues when we left to go upstairs. When we reached the main level, I said, 'Mom that means to go into all the world and preach the gospel' (Mk 16:15). I not only spoke in tongues, but I knew what the conversation was about. I have looked back to that time knowing the Lord called me and set me apart. I wouldn't have known that Scripture at so young of an age. It was a fluid prophecy that came from the prayer room.

> *"The Lord called me and set me apart as a little girl to know and speak His Word and preach the Gospel."*

"That encounter has been significant in my life."

Merodee also concretely experienced the Presence of God when she was young.

"When I was three or four, Dad read to me from a children's Bible. I can't recall the story, but I remember the picture. There were clouds with the sun's rays coming through. I studied the picture, sensing the invitation to have a relationship with God. The picture said, 'God came down from Heaven. He pours Himself out.'

"Even so young, I already knew my heart was lonely. Living in a family where love was lavished on me didn't quench the deep love I craved. I wanted whatever was in the picture. I wanted "it" inside of me.

"Afterward, I asked Mom a lot of questions. One day, she said, 'Do you want to invite Jesus to be your Lord and Savior?' I gladly received Him. Later that night, I crawled into bed knowing I wasn't lonely anymore. I was so aware of His Presence.

"Conversation with Him flowed as I prayed for whatever. I wanted a baby brother or sister, but Mom and Dad said, 'No!' Undeterred, I thought, 'No problem! I will just go above you guys straight to God.' I never prayed presumptuously and even prayed for my doll to come to life. God went through tradition-al venues, however. Whenever the thought of a baby brother or sister would bubble up, I just prayed in simple, childlike faith.

"One day when I was nine years old, Mom went into town, leaving us home with Dad. 'I think she's pregnant,' I told my sister, who agreed with me. Later, Dad and Mom called a fam-ily meeting, but before they could tell us, my sister and I said, 'Yes. We know you're pregnant.' It was so childlike.

"That kind of open, knowing prayer just flowed."

Perhaps we should eavesdrop on our children's prayers to be fore-warned of what they are partnering with God for. Never doubt the power of a child's prayer! Miranda has seen the results of persistent believing prayer. She is another example of God moving miraculously through the prayers of His little ones.

"I didn't pray a lot when I was little, but the main thing I prayed was for Dad to come back home. Dad wasn't living with us, but I wanted our family back together. I was about six years old when I started praying about it.

"I would also pray at school with one of my teachers. She would pull each of her students aside to pray with us individu-ally. Every time she did, I had the same prayer. 'God, bring Dad back home.' I don't even know if she remembers, but that was my only prayer, 'God, bring Dad back home.'

"My prayers were short—not too in-depth—just really simple.

"*They were simple prayers of trust.*"

When Dad came home, it was no surprise to Miranda. Even

though her parents had been separated and divorced for the better part of three years and had to work hard to restore their relationship, they *were* remarried. Miranda's family *is* together because one child refused to pray any other prayer except, "God, bring Dad back home." The prayers of a child are "short—not too in-depth—just really simple," but they are powerful and effective before God.

Mark shared a few of his childhood experiences, starting when he was about five years old.

"When I was a young child, my parents came to the Lord and were serious about their faith. From then on, prayer was the natural response to everything that happened in our home.

"When we lost something, we prayed. If someone hurt themselves, we prayed. When relationship problems arose, we prayed. We did repetitive prayers at meals and bedtime, but it was the spontaneous prayers which affected me the most.

"My mother's childlike faith especially challenged my own. She seemed to have bold, unwavering faith. Sometimes her prayers sounded like a prayer, but most of the time she talked to God like He was right beside her.

"My father suffered a severe illness; we weren't sure if he would recover. It was a scary time, but as a family, we circled together and prayed. God honored our simple prayers.

"I don't think my faith was great as a kid, but God answered my genuine childlike faith even before I came into a personal relationship with Him.

> *"Childlike faith believes without doubting; often in my doubting, I search to believe."*

Kristina shared,

"When we were thinking about starting homeschooling, God spoke through our son. For quite some time, we felt God might be asking us to homeschool, but we didn't know why. Neither of us had experience with homeschooling or had been homeschooled.

"We were wrestling with the decision because we were hoping to move out to our land. We didn't know whether the bank would approve us for a mortgage with only my husband's income. There were other variables to consider. We didn't know why God would ask us to homeschool, but it seemed like He was speaking to us more and more.

"One evening, Michael and I were sitting in our living room having a conversation about it. We had just tucked our kids into bed. He seemed to not be totally in favor of homeschooling, but I strongly felt like this was where God wanted us to head.

"I went into the bathroom and prayed, 'God, I really need you to speak to us and my husband.'

"When I came out of the bathroom, our son, who would have been five or six years old, was coming back down the stairs. Annoyed, I said, 'You need to get back to bed.'

" 'I'm scared.'

" 'What do you do when you're scared?' I asked, repeating the tips to him. He started heading up the stairs, and I went back to sit on the couch. I could hear him creeping downstairs again and I was getting exasperated.

41

"Halfway down the stairs, he said, 'I think God gave me something for you guys.'

"He came into the living room to talk to my husband and me. 'You know when you are looking at something in your head and it looks one way, but when you look at it with your heart, you get the answers?'

"We listened to him and watched as he went back upstairs. We knew in our hearts we needed to homeschool even though it made little sense in our logical minds or heads.

"It was a pretty cool answer to prayer. Out of the mouths of babes!"

At the same time, children will be children, as Karli's story shows.

"I thought God was up in the sky—no conversation needed. At seven years old, I went to vacation Bible school where they taught prayer as talking to God. A lady at the door asked if she could pray with me. She said, 'Do you want to accept Jesus today?'

"I thought she was a bit crazy. Then she explained more about accepting Christ into my heart and confessing Jesus with my lips. She prayed, and I followed. That was the first time anything prayer-like was opened to me.

"I was filled with questions afterward. I said, 'I want You to speak. Please speak to me. I want to hear You.' Then I put a journal and pen by my nightstand, expecting God to write something to me in the night. When I woke up the next day finding nothing written, I decided, 'God doesn't speak. He didn't write me back. He doesn't care.'

"When I was nine years old, I sometimes had a sleepover at

a Christian friend's place. Her mom would pray, 'Thank You, Lord, for . . . We ask for clarity and guidance with . . . Thank you, Lord, for rest and sleep.'

"I thought, 'Why does God speak to them and not to me?' I knew they prayed and saw things come to pass. I didn't understand how they were hearing from Him."

Many years ago, Lauren told me this story about her son. I asked her to share it with us.

"This is such a reminder of the Lord's faithfulness. All these years, God has protected and kept us. Our God is good!

"Every night when tucking our children into bed, we prayed, bowing our heads to thank God for His blessings in our lives. Each night, without fail, our son Levi prayed, 'Please keep fire off our house.' His request was always earnest and full of faith.

"One day when my husband had to repair the washing machine, he pulled the dryer out from the wall. He noticed the dryer plug area was charred. Upon further investigation, he realized that the wires would heat every time the dryer was used. It was clear this condition had been ongoing and repeated inside the wall behind the plug. We had occasionally smelled hot electrical scents and pulled the dryer out, but there was never anything to see as it was always inside the wall. However, that day it clearly showed what we had been smelling. Each load had created more charring.

"My husband was amazed it had not, on one occasion or another, ignited and created a fire.

"Answered prayers make kids into prayer warriors!"

"The Lord heard Levi's prayers. His amazing grace kept us safe."

Joy-Lyn also shared her story of encountering God when she was very young.

"I remember vividly when I was six or seven years old, sitting in bed reading about Solomon asking for wisdom from the Lord (1Kgs 3:9). It was late at night.

"The fact that Solomon recognized his need for wisdom caused me to have a revelation of the importance of wisdom in my life. I started crying because it hit me so powerfully. I said to the Lord, 'I just want wisdom. If I could have anything, it would be wisdom.'

"I didn't notice any significant changes in my life immediately, but looking back now and even currently, wisdom is the one thing that gets called out from my life more than anything else. Many people, even non-Christians, have said, 'You are wise for your age—wise beyond your years.'

"At that time in my life, I saw God as my Source. I recognized already the truth that God held everything and owned everything. He was my Source for strength, peace, comfort, and guidance. All I needed was in Him.

"That moment was perhaps one of the most significant God encounters I have had."

Though fundamental to our Christian walk, having a childlike faith is perhaps the hardest to regain once lost. The Bible challenges us to pursue maturity while also possessing a childlikeness in our relationship with God.

> **"Learn this well: Unless you dramatically change
> your way of thinking and become teachable,
> and learn about heaven's kingdom realm
> with the wide-eyed wonder of a child,
> you will never be able to enter in."**
> **Matthew 18:3 TPT**

Entering the trust of childlike simplicity is easier said than done. Nonetheless, childlikeness is essential to coming to our Heavenly Father in prayer. Like a little child, we can confidently hope in God, our Source and fullness of all that is good.

> **"You are good, and what you do is good . . ."**
> **Psalm 119:68**

His goodness and His God-ness are inseparable. Children receive and believe with an open heart the love of God. They absorb truth like sponges absorb water.

> *"Our children are prayer warriors. They have the innocence of faith to believe God. Often, the more we age, the less we think we need God." — Clay*

Adult reasoning and intellect can become the greatest obstacles to believing prayer. Prayer often sounds too simplistic for many adult-sized problems. A child, however, will believe biblical truths with unquestioning faith.

> **"And without faith it is impossible to please God,
> because anyone who comes to him must believe
> that he exists and that he rewards those who
> earnestly seek him."**
> **Hebrews 11:6**

Rachel's experience with God at a very young age proved common. Many other spoke of desiring to sense His Presence again, like they once did.

"From the time I was very young, even a year and a half old, I had an amazing relationship with God. I spoke to Him all the time and heard Him speak to me. Although I don't think it was audible, at times it felt like it. Often, I would forget about everything in the room except Him; no walls separated us; nothing blocked Him or His love; His Presence felt so close.

"A woman once told me about seeing this little girl, about two years old, standing on top of a pew, being held up by her mother. That girl was me! Apparently, for the whole service, I stood on the pew with my face and hands turned upward, reaching toward God. I don't know whether that means the entire service or only during worship. She was so surprised she kept her eyes on me the whole time. I don't remember doing it, but I believe it is true because of the longing I had for Jesus and the closeness I felt toward Him.

"Around five or six years old, however, fear and doubt came into my life. Then confusion and legalism took over. Even though I felt distant from God, I still held on to Him with hope. I knew beyond a shadow of a doubt He was the One I wanted to walk my life with. After experiencing His joy and love as a small child, there was no other One I wanted to follow.

"Sometimes when I've struggled in my relationship with God, instead of feelings of hopelessness, I've always known God is good. He is in control; He always wins."

I don't know of anyone who has cultivated a godly childlikeness as an adult as well as Karli. She combines this attribute with mature wisdom.

"Often in life when things go wrong, we turn somewhere else or to something else for help. I have learned how much easier life is when we turn to God first, trusting Him as opposed to going through a different, longer process. We can get off track by looking for the affirmation of others instead.

"When I began turning to the Lord with big or little things, even when things went wrong, He helped me and pulled me through. Each time, I grew deeper in trusting Him with child-like simplicity.

"Trust is not having all the answers while still stepping forward anyway. God has fostered in me a childlikeness paired with wisdom. Trusting my Heavenly Father can sometimes look like letting God have control of the situation.

"I lean back in Daddy's arms knowing He provides even when I don't understand. Honestly, I don't get it most of the time!

"I have a beautiful childlike relationship with the Lord, rooted in prayer and intimacy. God always comes through with His promises.

> *"I am the only one who can be me—childlike and free— catching some of the waves of His Presence others don't."*

"God sees the pieces I can't yet see. Trust is knowing who He is through His promises, which leads me to ask and seek more of His character.

"I can trust
    in the kindness of God,
        in the love of God,
            in the honor of God, and
                in the authority of God.

"The Bible says I am His child seated in the heavenly places

(Eph 2:6, Gal 3:26). I can ask God, 'What does this childlike quality bring to the world and Your people?' I rest knowing I am the only me around."

Amanda ⁵· teaches children both professionally and in ministry.

"Children are so aware spiritually, but they don't know how important that is. My husband and I were both spiritually alert as children. He regularly saw demons, while I often saw and talked to angels.

"As I grew up, I began to believe prayer was only for adults. They were the ones who had wonderful encounters with God. I didn't realize I was already having intimate encounters with God, too. Nobody told me I was hearing from God. I would often ask God for comfort and receive it.

> *"We forget to tell children how wonderful their experiences are."*

"We are getting better at teaching children how to know the difference between the voices of God, satan and themselves. Yet, many children still don't believe they will have those big moments in prayer until they are adults.

"I have received healing when kids have prayed for me. We need to remind them, 'God is working through you. Prayer is important!'

> *"We need to let children know their experiences with God are monumentally big."*

"We have had prophetic workshops with children where kids

accurately heard God's voice. Giving children exercises like that helps them develop their ability to hear and to know they are hearing from God. Prayer exercises can build their faith. Even when they don't hear right, we can help them use it as a learning experience."

During children's ministry, Kevin & Merodee have witnessed God speak and move in monumental ways. Kevin says,

"We would sometimes put worship music on. Half the kids would lie on their backs on the floor with their eyes closed and hands raised. Then we would ask them what they were seeing or hearing. Primarily, we heard about the depth of God's love for them or about the peace and comfort they experienced with Him.

> *"We have seen a massive revelation in kids as young as two years old."*

"On one occasion, Merodee decided to do prophetic coloring and drawing. I didn't realize this would be a powerful encounter, but it excited me to try it out. I was eager to see what would happen. Merodee told me to just start asking the children about their drawings. 'Ask questions until you get to the God thing they are doing,' she said. With some kids, it was a lot of questions; with others, it was only one.

"One two-year-old girl was scribbling on the page. I chuckled to myself when I walked over to her. 'What are you drawing?' I asked.

" 'Oh, angels,' the little girl said.

"I thought that was profound already, but her picture didn't look like anything. I asked, 'What are your angels doing?'

49

" 'My angels are drawing squares,' she said.

"I asked further, 'Why are the angels drawing squares?'

"This girl said, 'Well, I think it is because God never lies and neither does a square.'

"How did a two-year-old know a square doesn't lie? I have a carpentry background and own more squares than any guy needs. I understand well the purpose of a square is to establish true and perfect.

"I honestly think the Lord used that moment to show me how He moves in kids' lives. The language of children differs from our language; they see like we don't see. I need to expand my understanding of how and why God might do things in their lives.

"When we ask children questions, often the first answer is superficial, not the God answer. If we continue asking, we get to the thing God is speaking to them.

"There was also a young boy under five years old. He cried and cried because he couldn't draw what he saw. He was trying to draw a lion, 'The Lion of Judah,' he told us, 'He is roaring over the nations. When He roars, the dead come to life.'

"I thought, 'What! How old are you?'

"He wouldn't keep his picture because it didn't look like the image of what God had shown him. He described it further to us, 'The lion had his paw out front with his claws out.'

"That picture is probably my favorite painting."

Unmasking the Myth

An erroneous myth says, "Only adults need to take part in prayer!" It is the belief that children cannot speak to God, nor clearly hear His voice.

God is shaking my paradigm to believe to a greater degree how much children hear and see. They may even have a deeper connection with God than most adults or even seasoned prophets and prayer warriors today.

Dutch Sheets recently read a vision from Lana Vawser, an Australian prophet.[1] In part, Lana said, "I felt an excitement in my spirit. The King of Glory is stepping in . . . I saw the Lion of Judah positioned over the United States. He was HUGE with each one of His paws placed on the four corners of the United States . . . out of His mouth came a loud roar . . . As the roar of the Lion of Judah was released, I saw John 3:16 exploding. Everywhere the roar went, John 3:16 exploded up out of the ground . . . the King of Glory is stepping in."

John 3:16 says,

> **"For God so loved the world that he gave his one
> and only Son, that whoever believes in him
> shall not perish but have eternal life."**

She explained that the roar of the Lion of Judah was releasing life.

Do you recognize the similarity between what a young child, less than five years old, saw and what this acclaimed Christian prophet had also seen? The Lion was roaring, bringing the dead to life. Though the prophet saw the Lion stretched out over America, the child saw it stretched over all nations. She had the maturity to fill in a scriptural context with Bible verses that the young child did not yet know. They both saw the Lion coming with power and authority—with outstretched paw and claws.

It is astounding that God revealed to the child what He didn't show a major prophet until over two years later! Perhaps we should take the words of Jesus seriously,

> **"Jesus said, 'Let the little children come to me,
> and do not hinder them, for the kingdom of
> heaven belongs to such as these.' "**
> **Matthew 19:14**

I believe God has given us a responsibility to open opportunities for children to encounter Jesus Christ. Those God-moments with children can also teach us the childlike qualities He wants us to possess.

There are far more childlike attributes worth cultivating than this brief list, but it's a beginning:

- vulnerability and trust
- joyful abandon
- curiosity and wonder
- capacity for constant growth and learning
- willingness to forgive quickly and fully
- ability to love without reservation

After seventy-two follows of Jesus returned to report about their exploits in ministry, Jesus said,

> " . . . 'I praise you, Father, Lord of heaven and
> earth, because you have hidden these things from
> the wise and learned, and revealed them to little
> children. Yes, Father, for this is what you
> were pleased to do."
> **Luke 10:21**

These followers were mature people of faith who simply trusted and obeyed Jesus' commands. Yet, Jesus called them little children. As little children, their hearts and wills were submitted; they were filled with joyous wonder; their love for Jesus pushed them beyond preconceived spiritual norms. The result? It gave Jesus great joy!

No matter how old we become, pursuing not childishness, but childlikeness will reap many rewards. Here's a prayer to initiate the process,

> *"Heavenly Father, thank You for welcoming me as
> Your child. Today I place myself into Your sovereign
> care. Show me how to become childlike without being
> childish. Teach me how to approach You as my good
> loving Father and to trust You with childlike
> innocence. Restore the ability to live abandoned to You.
> I put myself in Your hands. Please lead me into greater
> childlikeness and faith in prayer with You."*

If children are a part of your life, you're blessed. Use daily opportunities to cultivate in them the confidence to hear God's voice for themselves and others by fostering prayer in their lives.

> *"Your kids see if you are faithful in prayer. I love the image*
> *of one hand embracing the child beside you and the*
> *other hand reaching out and embracing Jesus.*
> *We are a conduit between the two."*
> *— Caran*

If there is one thing that has become abundantly clear through these interviews, it is that children need to both hear and see us praying. Nothing replaces the modeling of prayer which occurs in our homes, churches, and youth groups. Personally living a life of prayer is the best way to teach children the significance and priority of prayer. Only God knows what will result!

> *"When you are a child, you have childlike faith.*
> *It's that simple. Faith is not rational.*
> *Faith is supernatural." — Caleb*

***

> *"Don't underestimate children!*
> *It is important to pour into kids concerning prayer."*
> *— Emily*

***

> *"Prayer is so simple the smallest child can do it but so complicated you cannot put it into words."*
> *– Sharon*

***

Notes

1. Dutch Sheets, "Prophecy!2019 Surge of Spiritual Power & Momentum + King of Glory Over U.S. Dutch Sheets," *VFNtv @ VFNKB.com, (VFN Kingdom Business: Business and Life Coaching),* YouTube video, 27:00, posted April 19, 2019, https://www.youtube.com/watch?v=sBPjZKvrOfo.

CHAPTER 4

Signals from Heaven – Sacred Echoes

> *"Knowing God's voice is like getting a phone call*
> *from an old friend you haven't spoken to in many years.*
> *The second you hear God speak you know who it is."*
> *– Mike*

After rushing through the morning chores and double-checking directions, I hurried off. The lengthy drive through open country settled and calmed my spirit. Wide expanses of prairie flatland invited me to breathe deep the fresh morning air.

Small groups of cattle milled around watering holes, while larger herds grazed unhurriedly through adjacent pastures. Welcome memories of decades spent on the farm ebbed and flowed through my thoughts as gentle as the soft summer breeze.

The gently rolling land transitioned between pastures and grain fields, then back again. The ripening fields of green and gold swayed effortlessly in waterless waves. God whispered, "Look at the fields! They are ripe for harvest."

As I drove, I prayed for both the natural and spiritual harvest, "Send out laborers, Lord, into the fields. The harvest is ready. It's good."

I once considered lengthy drives a waste of precious time. Everything changed when my car became a hub of prayer and worship. I also realized, after being issued a speeding ticket, that cruise control was for just these moments!

As I drove, songs of adoration freely ascended Godward from my overflowing heart. An excitement built within me as I approached the small, secluded Bible camp where I was headed. In the peaceful valley, towering elm and ash hung protectively over quaint cabins. The playful sounds of children punctuated the joy and anticipation I felt.

Since I was a stranger here, I began introducing myself to a small group of women sitting around a picnic table. Instantly, the conversation flowed naturally and easily.

A youthful woman sitting among other girls her age drew my attention. She met my gaze, stood and confidently strode across the yard toward me. As Charlotte introduced herself, her sparkling eyes, which perfectly reflected the deep blue sky, captivated my attention. What was the gem-like quality I recognized in her but could not yet identify?

Since hearing personal "God stories" is one of my favorite pastimes, I probed, "What is your story? Tell me about your relationship with Jesus."

Her long natural curly blond hair bounced with youthful fluidity, as she openly shared her journey to a recovery program for young women "to get her life straightened out." Self-harm in many forms had marked her few years. She swung her arms wide, exclaiming, "I never knew this existed! That God was real! That I could talk to Him and He would totally talk to me!"

The childlike abandon and wonder of fresh discovery seemed to flash through her countenance like a geyser refusing to be contained.

I couldn't help but laugh. "Yes, He 'totally' does. He is 'totally' real and He 'totally' speaks."

Now at eighteen, she was exploring this fresh world of faith— richer, deeper, and more fulfilling than she imagined. She was diving into a relationship with Jesus with wholehearted abandon. The erupting geyser of her contagious enthusiasm for God spilled out, drenching all of us and reminding us of the miracle of His Presence.

I knew, at that moment, she was the reason God brought me to this new place. He had an appointment for me to meet Charlotte.

For the rest of the afternoon, we chatted. A deep connection instantly joined us as sisters with the same Father,
learning the whispers of the God who loves,
discovering more about Jesus through each other,
seeking His face with hope for the future,
sensing the brush of the Holy Spirit,
stirring deep wells of life.

We know God used to speak through the Bible. Did the silent God grow suddenly chatty long enough for His words to be penned by prophets and scribes, then just as suddenly become silent again? People continue to question, "Does God speak today?"

"As Moses went into the tent, the pillar of cloud
would come down and stay at the entrance,
while the LORD spoke to Moses."
Exodus 33:9

God spoke to Jacob in a dream (Gn 28:12-15) and He spoke to Peter in a vision (Acts 10:9-16). A light blinded Saul and rendered him helpless, while a voice thundered from Heaven (Acts 22:6,7). God spoke to Balaam through a donkey (Nm 22:30) but spoke to and through His prophets in many other ways (Heb 1:1). Jesus spoke to the milling crowds using parables, but openly to His disciples. God is unrestricted in how He speaks, then and now.

> *"The question isn't, 'Does God speak?' The question is,*
> *'Will I listen when He speaks to me?' "*
> *– Staci*

The day I met Charlotte, there was no audible voice telling me where to go and what to do. No handwriting on the wall or dream with a roadmap directed my way. I only had this incessant stirring in my heart to go to a place I had never been before. Even as I went, I wasn't sure as to the reason for my going. It was an act of obedience to the faint nudge of Holy Spirit.

> **"I am the good shepherd; I know my sheep and my**
> **sheep know me . . . My sheep listen to my voice;**
> **I know them, and they follow me."**
> **John 10:14,27**

Personal Perspectives

So how did I know it was Holy Spirit? Good question! That's exactly what I asked those whom I had interviewed. Their answers were surprisingly consistent.

> *"Everyone encounters God in distinct ways, but everyone*
> *has that knowing. It is simple." – Emily*

The way God speaks is as diverse as the people I interviewed. Most people agreed with Mike,

> "As you grow in your knowledge and friendship with God, you just know His voice. I wouldn't say I function perfectly in hearing God's voice. I get that thought, or impression, and know it is Him."

Sometimes it takes someone like Charlene who is relatively new to prayer to remind us how amazing prayer is.

"Everything was so new because I didn't have a prayer life before. I watched a video which talked about getting into the prayer room—into the secret place with God. I thought, 'Okay! That's what I have to do.'

"I went into my room one day, sat on my bed with the curtains open so I could see the sky and just started talking to God. I heard nothing back—nothing. But I kept praying even though I didn't hear Him respond.

> *"I didn't realize He was there—He was with me. I was trying to figure out, 'Who are You, Lord?' "*

"The more I prayed, the more certain I became that Jesus was real. My prayer started changing. It was like a switch turned on in my brain—a revelation. 'He *is* real!'

"Then I knew I needed to get into my quiet room. I wanted to know who He was and to hear His voice, every single day.

"God would often speak to me through the Bible. In the beginning, He would tell me to go to page 985, or whatever page He wanted me to read. Whenever I read that portion, it would be, 'Wow, I needed that today!' I would take a red pen and draw a square around the verses. I was learning how to co-operate with His voice. Sometimes, He would point things out that He wanted me to know or focus on from the Bible. The words would literally 'pop out' at me like they were written and magnified in three dimensions.

"Now when I am reading, I say, 'Lord, speak to me. Show me what You want me to know.' Then I pray and meditate on those verses.

"About a year after I started praying, I was in my room speaking to God. I began to hear Him—just little bits, little bits, little bits. At first, it almost sounded like my voice, but He spoke with such love and encouragement. I knew if I was talking to myself, I wouldn't use that language.

"Then He would tell me things like, 'You will pray for Miss S. today and her ears will be opened.' His voice was confirmed through the outcome. I went to Miss S. and said, 'I heard God say your ears will be opened today.' When we prayed, she noticed an immediate difference in her hearing right away.

"When God speaks, He isn't pressuring or commanding. In a way, it is like my dad speaking to me. There's a confirmation in my spirit, 'Yes, that's what the Lord wants.'

> *"I decided in my heart*
> *to believe and to trust His voice."*

"Now I just know! The more I have trusted Him, the more precise and clear His voice has become. His voice is the calm, loving voice of my Father."

   Keegan also experienced the growing process of hearing and recognizing God's voice.

"When I was a teenager, I realized the relationship side of prayer and started hearing God answer when I prayed. They weren't audible answers, but I heard God's voice in my thoughts. He affirmed He heard me and conversed back to me.

"Around that time, I became involved in youth leadership, read my Bible daily and built on other spiritual disciplines, training myself to connect with God.

"There are three dominant ways God speaks to me. The first is audibly hearing His voice. The second is when I am praying for others. He usually gives me a picture and then the interpretation of the picture. I am growing in that area and getting a clearer understanding of what He is saying. The third is usually in devotion time through prophetic writing. I write as God is sharing, penning it out."

Amanda ^{S.} hears from God in a slightly different way.

"I learned about the connection between worship and listening. I soon became more excited to hear God's voice and what was on His heart for me and for others. Then I would dance it out of the place of worship.

"A while later, I was invited to join an accountability group with a few ladies of different ages. We did Bible studies, prayed and spoke words of revelation and prophetic encouragement over each other. We were learning how to discern God's voice more clearly.

"God began showing me how He speaks through the voices of others, especially through close friends who love you and have your best at heart. They love with God's love and speak the words He wants you to hear.

"Not long afterward, I began a season of hearing what I now call *sacred echoes*. God is unrelenting. He brings people into my life who say something that resonates with my spirit. When a pastor speaks the same word in a sermon, then I randomly overhear the same thing in a conversation in a crowded room or read it in a book, it is a confirmation of what God has already spoken to me earlier. It gets my attention so strong that I can't miss it. God makes His voice obvious."

BreAnn says,

"I've heard God's audible voice and had seasons when God spoke to me through songs or pictures.

"When I was considering dating and marriage, I wasn't sure if I should enter a relationship with Mike. I didn't want to go ahead unless I knew God's direction. I was writing in my journal and praying for wisdom. In the back of my head, I heard an audible 'Yes,' but I needed things black and white.

"God put people in my life who prayed for me during that time. Even random people on the street would speak confirmation. Their words broke down the walls that kept me from pursuing this relationship. There was even a lady we transported in the back of the ambulance who told me, 'I'm going to visit my husband. He is fifteen years older than I am.' She put her hand on mine and said, 'I wouldn't change it for the world.'

"One thing holding me back was the fact that Mike is fifteen years older than I. Only God would speak and confirm His word like that.

"I often see pictures, like a scene in my head, or animated images. I know it is God speaking something to me. God will give me vivid dreams that wake me up in the night. It's amazing!

"I will usually record the things I believe God is speaking or showing me and then pray over it. Often, God will use someone else to confirm what I have seen or heard. At other times, I just don't have clarity. Sometimes I can look back and know for sure it was God. You don't always know though, and that's okay.

"I didn't start out seeing visions and pictures, but I learned to trust Holy Spirit with these unfamiliar elements."

Heather is a superb example of someone who has her antennas up to hear God and sense His movements.

"Prayer is like sending out a radar ping. When it doesn't echo back, or it comes to us in a way we didn't expect, we don't know what to do. If it doesn't come back in 'English,' we think God hasn't said anything. It has to do with our perception, not His voice. He is speaking; we are not always hearing or receiving.

"Over about five years, I spent a lot of time in the Presence of the Lord. God revealed Himself more prophetically to me. I began to receive more dreams, visions, encounters and prophetic words, even though I wasn't asking specifically for them. That time alone with God opened things up to me spiritually. I am not sure whether He specifically wanted to communicate in that way or whether my receptors just increased from spending more time with Him.

"Prayer can often be like going on a mysterious adventure with God. There are many ways I get directions or hints from Him, like through the spiritual senses of seeing, hearing, smelling, tasting and feeling. Then, I must seek out what He is saying and what He wants me to do about it.

"One example is when I kept hearing an unfamiliar word, '*mogadishu*,' pop into my mind. I thought it might be a demonic word, or a curse, or something, so I kept praying against it in Jesus' Name. Finally, I looked up the word and realized, 'Oh, it's the capital of Somalia! I think I'm supposed to pray for something there.' I felt led to pray for the safety of missionaries in Somalia. About two years later, I ran into missionaries who had been in Mogadishu at that time. They told me a lot of Christians had been martyred during the time I was praying. It was an eye-opener for me concerning prayer, hearing God's voice and activation to intercede."

Shelly added another tried-and-true means of testing God's voice against our thoughts or even the devil's whispers.

"God will never contradict the Bible. He has placed His Word above His Name (Ps 138:2 KJV). Almost every time I missed it big was when I wasn't listening to God because of self-doubt. I thought, 'There's something wrong with me. I'm not hearing right.'

"I have made enormous mistakes by not following His peace. I have had checks in my spirit so strong I've felt like vomiting. The consequences of not heeding His voice have not been nice. It is comforting to know He was trying to speak to me. There can be great peace when I am listening to His voice and following Him, and an equally great lack of peace when I am not listening.

> *"There is a sense of peace that accompanies His voice."*

"Many times, other people will confirm to me—people I know or even online sermons. Often, I think, 'Did You write this just for me?' I know ten thousand people are listening, but it seems like this was written directly to me. Having godly relationships and mentors you can trust is so important to confirm God's voice."

Virtually all the people I talked with mentioned the importance of hearing confirmation, usually through other believers or the Bible. God not only speaks but will also confirm what He said through various means.

Isaac felt God's Presence tangibly.

"I said, 'Jesus if You are real, I want to feel You.' I instantly felt a blanket of peace. I wasn't expecting an answer because I had drifted so far away from God. The peace honestly shocked me. I said it again, 'Jesus, if You are real, I want to feel You,' and it happened again.

"A dusty Bible was sitting on my dresser. I knew I had to read it and to start seeking Jesus. I started getting involved in church, took discipleship classes and joined Master's Commission. I wanted to hear and know God more.

"I hear God mostly through thoughts and dreams, sometimes visions. I also see in my mind's eye. As well, He will lead me to the Bible to back up what I'm hearing and seeing.

"When I have thoughts or memories that stop me in my tracks, I know it is God. What I am reading in the Bible will be exactly what He was telling me earlier. Other times when I'm praying and reading my Bible, He will give me an illustration of what He is saying in His Word. Still other times His voice sounds more like a modern parable. In whichever way He chooses to speak, He will never go against His Word."

Often God surprises us with something unusual. A little while ago, I was sharing a room with a few ladies at a camp retreat. One woman arrived feeling worn out after an extremely difficult year. After evening service, she spent extra time praying and receiving prayer. Though she sensed some release, the strain of the past year continued to weigh on her.

She was young enough to be my daughter, and my heart was moved with deep compassion for her. Without thinking twice, I invited her to receive the comfort of a motherly snuggle. I desired to let her know she was loved and cared for.

As she drew close beside me, she began sharing the burdens still weighing heavy upon her. Suddenly her eyes grew big with excitement, 'Do you smell that? You have to be smelling it!'

Though I had caught a fleeting scent of something, it quickly passed me and hovered directly over her. She sprang upright, ecstatic with wonder. Aroma after aroma passed over her, burning her nostrils with intensity. She said if it had been a normal scent, she would have easily incurred a headache, but since it was a heavenly perfume, she bore no ill effects. The aroma changed several times before leaving.

Struggling to believe what she had experienced, she kept asking the rest of us if we were smelling anything. She couldn't imagine why not. "Come on! You have to be smelling it!" she said, "It's so strong."

Gradually the beautiful fragrance lifted and with it the heaviness she had experienced only moments before. She went around the room picking up various articles, trying to locate the source of the beautiful fragrance. The origin of the scent wasn't in something material, but in *Who* had visited her.

The funny thing was that the aroma had been infused directly into her. For some time afterward, she had scratch-and-sniff fingertips, and if she rubbed the ends of her fingers, a hint of the fragrance would again waft over her.

Only God would move in such a way upon His broken-hearted daughter to bring gentle healing and comfort. Only He could create such a joyous way to bring soothing restoration and relief.

Sometimes our encounters with God are sweet and supportive. At other times, He speaks words of correction. But always He is gentle and loving.

> *"God's voice is clear. It isn't loud, but it's clear that it's God speaking. There is wisdom in His words that isn't my thinking or imagination. It's the quiet voice of Holy Spirit speaking to me."*
> *— Jewell*

Dawn tells her story,

"Sometimes God speaks a brief statement through my mind. I know it's Him. At other times, He will give me a promise I know I would never say. On one occasion I was sitting in a chair praying. I hadn't asked Him for anything, but I heard Him say, 'I want to do something different through you and your husband.' I knew that thought wasn't mine. The words landed into my spirit. His words are Spirit to spirit, usually coming when I'm alone.

"We were going through a time of rest after a ministry period. I made a declaration out loud that I would trust God more,

> " 'Lord, I feel I can trust You enough to ask You to show me the error of my ways.' "

"I heard nothing. For several days I repeated, 'If there is anything I need to repent of, show me clearly the things I did wrong.' Several more days passed. I was feeling anxious about going back to work, and my spirit was unsettled. I was cross with my husband and upset with myself.

"In my quiet time, God brought me to Ephesians 4:2, '**Be completely humble and gentle; be patient, bearing with one another in love.**'

"I felt compelled to write it out the opposite way. 'Lord, make me not impatient. Help me not be proud but gentle, not aggressive or hard, not hateful. Lord, free me from impatience and anger when I don't get my way. May I not have an uncontrolled tongue or words of strife. Take away all negative attitudes.'

> "There is no flowery talk around the Lord. He speaks beautifully, shortly and succinctly."

"I knew immediately it was the Lord revealing the error of my ways. I repented and heard Him say, 'There is more of Me, Dawn, to pour out to others. There is more, Dawn.'

"I focused on impatience and saw what impatience had cost me. God is so loving. He doesn't say, 'Don't do that! Stop doing that!' When God corrects, it is so sweet and gentle. He shows why this doesn't serve us or Him in any way. It isn't about right or wrong.

> *He spoke so quickly as soon as my heart reached out to Him. He doesn't leave His kids hanging.*

"I used to sit outside on my deck and watch the birds. I'm amazed at how God made birds so different—some industrious, others vicious. He made such a variety! I had a dream one night about five years ago. In the dream, the words, 'Little Bird' were spoken. When I awoke, I said, 'Little Bird, that's the name God has given me.'

"When I first came to the Lord, I would hear Him say, 'My Daughter,' giving me a sense of belonging. That was so important in those days.

"God gives us what we need even when we don't know what we need. When we experience the depth of how He builds our identity, it is foundational."

God speaking through visions impacted Yogeswari's life, resulting in people turning to Christ.

"When I pray, I call God my Daddy. 'Daddy, please come; I want to talk with You; I'm waiting for You; Daddy, give me Your thoughts. I want Your anointing.' Only with Holy Spirit anointing will I know what to pray for. I'll start praising God. When the Holy Spirit comes, I feel a burden and the heat of His Presence.

"I also ask God to give me His words to pray. I don't say, 'I need this or I want that.' I praise Him, praying in tongues. He is the Lion of the tribe of Judah, the Son of David.

"At four-thirty in the morning on December 26, 2004, I wasn't able to sleep and my heart felt very burdened. Feeling pushed to pray, I went into another room. With open eyes, I saw in a vision a beach filled with water. The temples and churches were falling, and cars were floating in the water. I could see a lot of dead bodies.

"I thought it might be a flood, so I asked Jesus, 'Should I pray about this flood?'

"When Jesus told me to look up, I noticed it was a bright sunny day. Then I knew it wasn't a flood from rain, but I still didn't know how to pray. I started crying and couldn't console myself, yet didn't know the reason I was crying. My heart was completely burdened and my throat filled with pain, but I didn't understand why. I couldn't concentrate on anything else. Whatever it was, it wasn't good. I could only weep. Though I could hardly speak, the only thing I knew to do was to pray in tongues and praise the Lord.

"Later, I called my Mom and shared the vision with her. She said, 'Everything will be fine. Go back to sleep.'

"At eight-thirty she called me back. She learned from the television news that a huge tsunami had hit Indonesia and India. Most of the people around the seashore, the churches, temples, and cars, were swept out to sea. Thousands of people died.

"I ran down toward the beach even though people were running away from the tsunami yelling, 'Don't go! Water is gushing! Water is gushing!' I knew I had to pray at the place where the tsunami was. Somehow, I wasn't afraid and knew nothing would happen to me.

"When I went there to pray, I saw exactly what God had shown me in the vision. I still didn't know what a tsunami was, and did not understand what was going on. I was confused and cried, 'Why did You show me? With so many deaths, didn't I pray well? What do You want me to do, Lord?' Even though I prayed, so many lives were still lost.

> *"It might be someone else's problem,*
> *but in prayer, it is my burden."*

"Because of the vision and the way God was answering many of my prayers, my Mom believed who I was worshiping was the only true God. She became a Christian too."

When God speaks, He speaks directly to our identity. Many people told me of special names God calls them, including
Warrior Child,
Little One,
My White Stallion,
Little Dove,
Dearly Loved Child.
Each name speaks identity and belonging.

God speaking in an audible voice was far more common than I expected. He spoke to Emily audibly, affirming her identity.

"I was struggling with how my future would turn out. I had some big tests to write and felt a lot of pressure. I stopped studying and began to worship God.

"I heard the audible voice of God say my name. I was terrified,

70

not in fear, but awe. The fear was like no other fear, yet I felt completely safe. I had been worshiping loudly, but as soon as I heard my name, I looked around and scurried to my bedroom. I stayed still, listening. Again, Jesus spoke, 'I am your inheritance.'

"Something clicked! I had been reading in Colossians about inheritance and thought, 'Jesus is my inheritance.' Since I have inherited Jesus, He is my future and abides in me. My future is secure because He is my inheritance. When thoughts come back and I wonder what is next, I remember Jesus is my inheritance.

"I wish I could tell everyone, 'Make plans for your future, but make all your plans in Jesus before you make your plans anywhere else.' "

But there are many more ways God speaks.

"God is a supernatural God. He doesn't want us running from one experience to another, but desires to speak to us through His Word. I have seen words written like ticker tape rolling in front of my eyes." – Joy

Audrey talked about hearing God in a way new to her.

"In Master's Commission, we were practicing words of knowledge. Pastor Graham told us to ask the Holy Spirit to give us the middle name of the person next to us. We started praying. I'm supposed to get the middle name of the man sitting to the right of me. All I could think about was a lady I knew from Quebec. I wasn't sure why I was thinking about her, so I pushed those thoughts away and tried to stay focused.

"Suddenly, into my head I saw written on a screen coming in through one temple and going across the inside of my forehead the words, 'Emma Louise.' I spoke it out. Emma, who was sitting on my far left, screamed, 'How did you know that?' I wasn't even asking for her middle name, but of course, that was her middle name. I had no idea!

> *"God will show you it is Him!"*

"Meanwhile, the man next to me revealed his middle name was Claude. Then I knew why I was being reminded about the lady from Quebec—that was her husband's name. I was trying so hard to push the thoughts away, but it was God speaking to me."

Recently, I held a miniscule part of Caran's *sacred echoes* from God at a Christian writer's conference. She graciously permitted me to include her testimony expounded on her website caranjantzenwrites. com.[1]

"In the center of a sepia-tone room void of detail, there stood a solitary figure, cocooned in a silken sheath. The figure straightened up with outstretched arms and dropped the gauzy cover to the floor. It was naked and unashamed with pure perfection. As I continued to watch, the figure twirled in place, spinning until up from its sides, from its very being, lifted a rippling skirt that danced in waves as the figure continued to twirl around. All at once, as if a curtain dropped, the image of the twirling figure with its rippling skirt went black. The vision was over.

"For weeks I pondered the vision. Was it me in Heaven made perfect in His Presence? As weeks became months, I thought less about what this vision meant. I doubted I would ever know.

"Months later, I found myself at my first-ever writer's conference. Armed with pens and notebooks, I was ready to glean as much wisdom and practical knowledge as I could from my fellow writers and published authors. I couldn't wait for what God had in store for me that weekend. My anxious thoughts melted away as I mingled and met fellow writers.

"I quickly learned all these men and women loved Jesus with their whole hearts. They were unashamed of the Gospel and were passionate to share His love through their writing. On more than one occasion, I felt I was standing on holy ground as we worshiped collectively together.

"I realized God hadn't just led me to this weekend writer's conference to learn how to improve my craft, He had brought me here to draw me into a deeper relationship with Him. This realization culminated on the last day of the conference, beginning with my quiet time before early morning prayer.

"As I was praying and listening in the quiet of my room, a refrain from a verse floated into my head, 'He rejoices over you with singing.' I didn't have time to look up the Bible reference as I was already late for our prayer gathering. The message of God rejoicing over me filled me with so much joy, I practically skipped down the steps to the prayer meeting.

"Each member who gathered around the table shared their prayer requests. My request was to continue to take time to meet with God despite my busy life. That morning as I shared, my heart ached to find peace and rest against the bosom of Jesus; tears spilled over as we prayed.

"New friends prayed over me as the Lord led them in ways only He could have done. They knew nothing of my circumstances, and yet the Lord gave them the exact words to pray. He reminded me again His mighty Spirit is constantly at work among His people.

"Later that morning, our worship became a beautiful picture of unity as God's people joined together. Before I knew it, the day, and the conference, had come to a close. One member rose to give a final benediction before we would head back to our homes scattered across the country.

"She read,

> **"The LORD your God is with you, the**
> **Mighty Warrior who saves. He will take great**
> **delight in you; in his love he will no longer rebuke**
> **you, but will rejoice over you with singing."**
> **Zephaniah 3:17**

"Rejoice over me with singing! This was the verse God had placed in my mind that morning.

"Afterward, I shared this with a newfound friend. Shocked by her response, tears welled up in my eyes yet again. She shared that the meaning of God singing over us is that He literally twirls over us in His delight for us. Twirls? My mind instantly recalled the image in the vision I had had months earlier. Could this be the interpretation? The Lord was twirling over me in His delight for me?

"My heart was wrenched open in agonizing soul-satisfying love as He poured into me yet again that day. God's message for me was that He, in His pure perfection, takes delight in me, His daughter. He rejoices over me in singing and twirling. There is no shame in His Presence.

"I still marvel at how God handcrafted that day as He spoke into my heart. Not only were my writing passions and gifts affirmed, but He also affirmed me as His dearly loved child, daughter of the King of kings . . ."

Unmasking the Myth

You might ask, "Is this prayer? Is hearing God's voice a part of prayer?" A prevalent myth says only a chosen few pray and hear God respond. This myth extinguishes the expectation for everyday people like us to hear God's voice.

Does God still speak? It isn't just the witness of all these voices that declare, "Yes, He does!" The Bible verifies it, too.

**"For God does speak — now one way, now another
— though no one perceives it."
Job 33:14**

Did you catch it? God doesn't have a problem speaking; we have a problem hearing. My confidence comes from Jesus' words,

**"My sheep listen to my voice;
I know them and they follow me."
John 10:27**

I can relate to what Jesus is saying. While farming, I enjoyed taking care of livestock and discovering the unique personalities and individual quirks they each possessed. I often talked softly as I walked among them. My animals developed an element of trust in me but would become uneasy and flee from a stranger. My cattle knew my voice.

How much more can we, God's children, learn to recognize and discern His voice. God initiates and welcomes a two-way conversation with us. So instead of the myth that we should not or could not communicate with God, the opposite is true. God invites communication and makes His voice known. We only need to prepare ourselves to listen.

> *"God still speaks. It is a tragic void when believers don't believe God still speaks to us." – Caran*

Here is a handful of practical tips to help us learn to hear and know God's voice:

1. The Bible is the chief way God speaks and confirms His voice.

Therefore, it's important to know God's Word.

2. Learning to hear God's voice requires time. God can break into our busyness, but He often waits for us to turn toward Him, intentionally listening.

3. Approach prayer time with an expectation to hear from God. You may or may not hear anything the first time, but He will speak.

4. Record the impressions you see, hear or feel. Pray about them and ask other godly people for their feedback.

Discovering and discerning the character of those we love develops through spending time together. There is no substitute for spending time with God either. In His Presence, we become increasingly familiar with His goodness and love for us.

> *"Lord I want to know Your voice as clearly as I know the voices of the people I love. Open my ears to hear You, my eyes to see You, and my mind to comprehend what You are saying. I invite You to make Yourself known in whatever way You want. Increase the expectation and anticipation of Your Presence within me as I seek to know You more."*

> *"I have heard God as a small voice in the back of my mind. It is like my spirit is getting an impression and I suddenly understand better." – Amanda* C.

***

> *"One word from God will change everything."* – Pearl

***

> *"You just know it is God's voice. It is an inner knowing.*
> *Sometimes it is like a quiet voice inside;*
> *sometimes an impression or a dream."*
> *— Karin*

Notes

1. Caran Jantzen, Adapted from "He Delights Over You with Singing: A Writing Conference Life no Other." October 2, 2019, https://www.caran-jantzenwrites.com/author/caran-jantzen/.

CHAPTER 5

Modeling & Mentoring – Footprints

> *"I learn more by experience and watching others than by reading a book. I had people pattern prayer for me, but there could be even more mentors."*
> *– Shelly*

Since prayer had been non-existent in my family's life, I had no compass point to guide me as a young adult new in my relationship with Jesus. I was a helpless spiritual baby.

Initially, prayer was childlike and free. At other times, it was confusing. I was walking blindly into this unfamiliar territory. Like Jesus' disciples, I asked, "Teach me to pray." Amid the uncertainty, I often questioned, "Is this prayer?"

He wooed me into an ever-deepening relationship,
    filled me with excitement at each answer to prayer,
        pushed me through areas of difficulty,
            and encouraged me along the way.
I found inspiration within the pages of my Bible from the words

and actions of the greatest prayer mentors of all time, like Moses, David, Daniel, Jesus, Paul, and others. I highlighted prayers I read in the New Testament, memorizing them and praying them back to God.

Early on, I entered a season of intense travail in prayer, although I had no words for it then. It included spending lengthy periods on my face weeping fervently before the Lord for the souls of the lost—not just people I knew, but globally over nations. The burden to pray for lost souls felt weighty, as if pressing upon my chest. One day I said, "God, please take this burden away. It's too much!"

To my regret, God answered. Without a prayer mentor to guide me through that season, I lacked wisdom and understanding of intercessory prayer. How does one effectively bring the needs and concerns of others to God, without carrying the weight? How do you bring each request one-by-one, leaving it all with Him?

When I began attending church, multiple pieces in my prayer puzzle filled in. By watching and listening to other seasoned intercessors, I learned so much. They walked with authority in the Spirit and possessed a maturity for which I longed.

During a visit with a senior saint, she invited me to a time of prayer. Under a genteel veneer, a mighty warrior crouched ready! Although barely four feet tall, she proved to wield enormous authority in the Kingdom of Heaven. In one moment, she humbly approached her Master; the very next she had the devil groveling in the dust, kicking him in the teeth. She drew on the Word of God with razor-like accuracy, slicing between good and evil, God and man. Before me knelt a ferocious warrior effectively taking territory for God and thrusting every opposing force into oblivion. It was an experience I'll never forget; one that forever changed my prayer strategy.

Paul said,

> **"Whatever you have learned or received or heard**
> **from me, or seen in me — put it into practice.**
> **And the God of peace will be with you."**
> **Philippians 4:9**

I may not have been in the presence of Paul, but I knew I was in the presence of a Holy Spirit led intercessor. I also knew the pattern she had established for me was worth emulating.

Since then, I have prayed with many powerful prayer models and mentors. Some connections with these mighty prayer warriors were brief and momentary; others lasted decades.

God continues to connect me with people of prayer. Their examples inspire and propel me. With an open heart and teachable attitude, I've learned from the powerful example of others. I am grateful for every encounter with godly mentors and prayer models. Some of them have been small children, others much older; all have influenced my prayer life.

Personal Perspectives

Shortly after Kevin accepted Christ into his life, he started working for Dave, a local carpenter. Dave immediately started teaching Kevin the way to a vibrant and effective Christian walk, including daily Bible reading and prayer.

Kevin states,

"Even though I tried to pray every day, prayer felt awkward and made little sense to me at first. In a structured way, I would get down on my knees, fold my hands and pray by my bed. I would go through a list of everybody I knew and loved. I wanted everyone to experience God in the same way I did, so needs and people consumed most of my prayer time.

"In my first season of prayer, I prayed a lot for loved ones, especially my younger brother with whom I had always been close. We were both going through a discouraging time. He was searching for answers too. I pleaded, 'I've heard from You, God. Do the same for my brother.'

"I had an interesting prayer encounter early on. Pastor Ted, who had a powerful prayer life, held Tuesday and Wednesday morning prayer meetings. Since I couldn't work at the time and didn't have other distractions, I threw myself into those prayer meetings.

"One day at a meeting, I had my eyes closed praying. Two people came in, but I didn't look to see who they were. They prayed so beautifully and powerfully. One of them started to laugh and continued to laugh. For almost half the prayer meeting, she laughed.

"I knew the woman who had come in. After the prayer meeting, I asked her about laughing. 'Sometimes when I pray, I feel the joy of the Lord,' she said. 'It washes away all anxiety and fear.'

"Wow! Though I had experienced comfort from God, I had never had a release from the things I feared.

"By going to those prayer meetings, I started realizing prayer was an intimate encounter with God. I could bring anything to God? I could laugh before God? Are you kidding me? I don't have to be super serious? This woman's laughter stunned me, but it also was a foundational piece for my prayers.

> *"I didn't know it, but I was learning to pray with the powerful intercessors from our church."*

"God had set me on a neat path of learning. Those experiences with others in prayer shaped a lot of my prayer life. Intercession is an enormous part of my prayers now.

"I never know what my prayer time with the Lord will be like. Sometimes I have to leave the house and get into the car undisturbed where I might laugh, release a war cry or weep before God.

"Rather than being taught, I observed what normal prayer looks like, through listening and watching intercessors. Those ladies weren't strange but functioned normally in society. They had a connection with God I knew was worth pursuing. 'This is fantastic!' I thought.

> "The key to a prayer mentor is seeing the
> fruit of answered prayer."

"My best prayer mentor is my wife. Her life of prayer has been an encouragement and challenge to me. She probably has two hundred and fifty yellow Sticky Notes with names of people she is praying for. There are times and seasons when she goes into her war room until things shift. Her life of prayer has been the most consistent example I could imagine. There is something about learning from someone whose prayers are fruitful. When prayers are fruitful, they match the heart and will of God.

"My wife makes notes in her prayer journal, then she checks off and documents the answers. The most powerful modeling of prayer is when people pray and teach us to pray. Then they bravely share God's answers, even when those answers look different from what they had thought.

"I ask everyone I am mentoring, 'What captivates you in prayer? What are the things you often return to in prayer? Who are the people you pray for regularly?'

"I am thankful my journey is unusually blessed with mentors and models in prayer."

Jewell also has prayer mentors.

"Senior ladies in our church modeled the importance of daily prayer. They encouraged me to set aside time to pray. Prayer didn't need to be as long as theirs, but they taught me to be purposeful. They demonstrated how older women should teach younger women. Their prayers were serious and intentional, not just bullet prayers. They talked about their prayer lists and the results they were seeing.

"My husband is the best example of prayer. Especially in winter when farming is quieter, he prays for a couple of hours every day, consistently praying for others.

"I wasn't always as thankful for his prayers as I am now. When our children were small, I would say, 'Don't you have work to do? I have work to do. How can you just sit there and pray?' Though he didn't seem visibly productive, I realize now he was doing the most important work—praying.

"The entire family, and even extended family, have benefited from my husband's prayers. There have been so many changes because he was diligent in prayer. I know God's hand has been on our family because of his faithfulness to pray.

"It has been a great comfort to know he was covering me in prayer. His example taught me how to pray consistently and intentionally. We now enjoy a beautiful time of refreshing together as we meet weekly with a prayer group from our church."

Often the example of parents was the greatest modeling. Lowell shared his experience.

"The person who most significantly impacted my life was my father. Dad was a big believer in prayer and would always say the Lord's Prayer. As a family, we would say it out loud together.

"Both my parents modeled prayer with us and for us. I saw prayer was important to them. They grew up with multiple siblings on farms without electricity or other conveniences. If something happened, they prayed. They often experienced healing and saw God do significant things.

"Dad, Mom and four boys were in my family. When we prayed together, we all prayed out loud, simultaneously, not one at a time as most people do.

"Mom and Dad taught us about having a personal relationship with God—speaking to Him for ourselves, reading the Bible and doing devotions. Those habits were important for them to instill in us.

"Dad's strong spiritual leadership in our home made a sizeable difference in my life. When I was under ten years old, I often had major fevers. I remember Dad praying for me exactly as Elisha did in the Bible (2 Kgs 4:34). Scenarios like that affected my prayer life.

"I grew up seeing God do miracles as a result of prayer."

Patrick's mother taught him the Lord's Prayer, but in a slightly different way.

"My Mom was the one who taught me the Lord's Prayer. She showed me how it is complete and how I could use it as a model to guide prayer. First was recognizing I was praying to the One and only God. Then it was an example of being intentional with every line, asking for needs to be met, seeking and offering forgiveness, and then aligning my will to God's. When I wasn't sure what to pray, I could turn to the Lord's prayer and go from there."

Both Joy-Lyn's parents modeled prayer for her as well. Some of her earliest memories are of her dad praying.

"Dad is the reason my communication with God looks like it does. The way he prayed had a lot of influence on my life. As a little girl, under five years old, I sat in my booster seat in the back of the car hearing Dad pray.

"He prayed, 'Dear Jesus, this and this and this . . .' After a silent pause, he would talk again. I sat listening and watching my dad. He was having a conversation with nobody I could see. I knew he was praying, but I would still ask him, 'Dad, who are you talking to?'

" ' I'm talking to Jesus,' he would say, 'I'm praying.'

"I knew the answer, but I still asked anyway. Dad would say something and there would be a pause. Then he would say something else and there would be another pause.

"Some people struggle with their prayers being a checklist they need to get through rather than being conversational. Other people struggle with not praying enough, although who determines what enough is? Sometimes, I feel guilty about how informal and personal my prayers are.

"Once you make prayer a religion of requirements, it is no longer about a relationship. Prayer is Holy Spirit led. It is out of His prompts we pray for people and things. For some people, lists work, but for me, it is conversational like my dad modeled.

> *"God is my Father. Because I had such a good father,*
> *I saw God represented so often and so well*
> *through my earthly father."*

"I never felt like I lacked the voice of my Heavenly Father because Dad modeled that so well. God has used my dad to teach me to pray. God has also often spoken to me through my dad."

The image of a praying father and grandfather is permanently fixed in Lois' mind.

"Though they were busy farmers living a tough life, they always gave God first place and glory for everything. They prayed for family and others daily.

"At four or five years old, I would go to my dad's bedroom door, opening it a crack. Every morning and night my dad would be on his knees beside his bed praying. I had the highest respect for his prayer time.

"I can remember my grandfather at the kitchen table with his head bowed. He began every prayer with, 'Our loving Heavenly Father.'

"That example of prayer had a tremendous impact on me, not just in giving God first place, but setting a heart posture of submission to the Lord by kneeling in prayer."

Candice said,

"Until recently, I didn't have a mentor for prayer. Pastor Graham is the most prayer-oriented man I have known. I've had pastors who mentored in prophecy and other gifts, but never in prayer.

"I'm learning the importance of taking the Word of God, then speaking and praying it out. Because I'm praying the Word that doesn't move, I need to do it and keep doing it until I see the changes.

"Graham and Deb have helped me see prayer is not something we do, but who we are. It's something we are made to do. It's our life calling.

"I spent many years feeling lonely on the outside. I didn't have a strong circle of people to pray with, but I see God is gathering His people. The Lord has brought me into this prayer community with other psalmists, worshipers, and people of prayer. He has brought me out of the lonely wilderness into a lush prayer fellowship.

"God takes the solitary and sets them in families. My prayer journey started long before He connected me with people of prayer, but I am thankful for this season."

Caleb says,

"My dad taught me about prayer. He is the one who drove the point home that prayer is about a personal relationship with God. The only thing my parents did, regarding seeking help, was pray. As long as I can remember Mom has woken up at five in the morning to pray and have devotions. She has fasted and prayed one day a week since she was eighteen years old.

> *"I didn't realize I was following my dad and mom. I just did what they did."*

"While growing up I thought, 'Whatever!' Now I know what an impact they had on me."

Merodee's mention of her parents' prayers over thirty times in our interview speaks for itself.

"I can remember waking up hearing Dad in the little room praying. He would often be on his knees, bent over his Bible.

He never shushed me away, but I had to respect what he was doing. Even though I was too little to pray, I would get on my knees and rock, like my dad as he was praying in the Spirit. I heard him ask for wisdom and how to farm in a drought.

"I felt drawn to pray the way he prayed. Even then I knew there was something special about my father's prayers. I always wanted to emulate my dad in every way. I would even take my Bible and underline it like he underlined his.

"I saw the contrast between the travail and the peace. I witnessed the angst with which the prayers were lifted upward to God and the peace my dad walked in the rest of the day. I knew that contrast had to do with his time spent in prayer.

"I loved his lifestyle of prayer. Dad's ebb and flow of life requirements did not make regular times of prayer easy. Prayer wasn't a discipline he could rigidly keep, but it impacted me as he gave himself to it as often as he could. Dad prayed in all circumstances—the cab of his tractor or the pasture he was fencing. During day-to-day tasks, he allowed himself to come under the influence of Holy Spirit in prayer.

"Dad had a unique way of taking the Word of God, allowing the Holy Spirit to form it into a story and then telling those stories back to God. He prayed, friend to Friend.

"Dad was never ashamed to pray.

> *"Through example, Dad taught me there is an element of prayer that requires us to lay down our fear of man."*

"Mom loved praying in the Spirit and was unashamed about praying that way. She prayed boldly!

"Though I had been baptized in the Holy Spirit and felt moved to pray like my mom, I never did as a child. In high school, my sister and I rolled the car. Because it had been our example, we instantly both began praying in the Spirit. As soon as crisis hit, praying in the Spirit welled up from deep inside."

Godly parents paved a smooth path for Charlotte's prayer walk.

"My parents both had significant faith in the Lord. Every morning, my mother would spend time in the Bible with a notepad beside her, reading and praying. Even though she was a busy wife and mother, she believed teaching her children about Jesus Christ was her responsibility. She refused to leave this important aspect to others. Every night she spent about half an hour teaching us about Jesus and praying with us.

"On bended knees at the side of my bed with my Mom, I asked Jesus into my heart to wash away my sin and take me as His own. Even though I was only four years old, I can remember that night so well.

> *"It was just as if Heaven exploded."*

"From that moment on, my life was wonderfully different. I didn't live a faultless life, but I always knew God was there for me. Even as a little girl, prayer became very important to me.

"Although we didn't know it, we were very poor. Often Dad didn't have enough money to put gas in the car, but somehow, he would make sure to take us to the little church in town.

"Dad had grown up in Ireland where memorizing sections of the Bible in school was common. The Word of God seemed to flow from him, whether we were out digging potatoes, having supper in the field or sitting around the kitchen table. He would recite entire blocks of the Bible to us and help us to learn God's Word.

"Because of the encouragement of my mother and father, I wanted to pray and learn more about Jesus and the Bible. I was so glad I started memorizing Bible verses—hiding God's Word in my heart. Those verses keep coming back to me, sometimes to encourage, sometimes to scold, but always to lead me closer to the Lord I love.

"Because my parents honored God by instilling these things in us, it became meaningful to us for the rest of our lives."

Even though many people didn't have the example of praying parents, they expressed the tremendous impact mentors had on them. Emily says,

"When I was in Grade 7, our youth pastor gave us each a piece of paper teaching us how to pray using our hand. The thumb reminded us to pray for our family, the pointer finger stood for our leaders, the middle finger represented our friends, the fourth finger was for the sick and the pinky finger was for ourselves.

"He encouraged us to go home and pray for five minutes a day. I sat down with the sheet of paper in front of me, closed my eyes and prayed for twenty minutes. I loved it! When I came back to my youth leader, I was so excited. Unfortunately, my youth leader didn't believe me or share my excitement.

"Gain from others, but focus on Jesus."

"I didn't let it bother me and kept the excitement in my heart. That little exercise of talking with God without distraction sparked something in me for prayer."

91

Other Christian women set an excelleny prayer example for Helen.

"The women at Aglow modeled prayer for me. I knew they had a deeper prayer life than I had. These were women twenty or thirty years my senior. I always felt drawn to older people because I knew they had something I wanted and needed. There was a richness in their lives I couldn't deny.

"Ultimately, everyone has to find that path of prayer themselves."

"I loved ministering to other women through prayer after I learned better how to pray for others. I knew God had called me to prayer. Eventually, I later became the provincial prayer co-ordinator helping other women become more effective in prayer."

Kate learned more about prayer through others in her church family.

"I was hungry to gain an understanding of prayer and communicating with God. There were people in the church modeling prayer. They spoke to the Heavenly Father personally as if He was sitting right beside them in the room. They talked to the Lord on behalf of others honestly and enjoyed communicating with Him. That intrigued me.

"I listened carefully to them as they prayed and asked questions. I wanted to find out more and become a student of prayer. When I wasn't satisfied with their answers, I would talk to God about it. Often, random books would be given to me that answered what I needed to know. The Holy Spirit was my teacher, teaching me everything I needed to know about prayer.

> *"God is Lord of prayer. Prayer is all His doing."*

"I learned early on to rely heavily on the Holy Spirit's Presence within me. The ministry of the Spirit fascinated me. I wanted to learn every bit of Scripture that spoke about Him. The way He was leading me was also fascinating to me."

Clay felt he needed to circle the globe in his search for prayer mentors.

"I remember leading board meetings at our church. Each meeting started with a half-hour of praying. After five minutes, I was anxiously looking at my watch thinking, 'Let's get on with business.' I'm the last person who should be a prayer person.

"The church was going through spiritual challenges and people were leaving. I wanted nothing to do with spiritual warfare. We had other people on staff for that. I wasn't sure if I even believed in spiritual warfare and thought the enemy didn't exist.

"It was a crisis moment in my life. I recognized it was the godly older men in our church who were doing the spiritual battles in prayer. I asked God to open the door for discernment so I would know what to do. My prayer journey was birthed out of that crisis point.

"A few months later, I resigned. Since God was calling me to pray, I expected to be involved in a prayer ministry in my local church. I took a four-month journey traveling around the world learning how to pray from others.

"I identified ten people who I wanted to meet with. All were key prayer people whom I had read about. I searched out those who knew their authority, were bold in prayer and had great faith in what God could do and would do.

"Revelation 12 talks about the testimony of others. I knew I could learn from and build on the testimony of others who were powerful in prayer. So that's what I did."

A girl's club leader became a strategic prayer model for Jan.

"In Pioneer Girls, our group leader helped us put a phone number for a prayer line on all the cars outside of a hotel. Then we would volunteer to sit by the phones, ready to pray for whoever called. At eleven or twelve years old, I would go to the church right after school to answer the prayer calls when they came in.

"During evenings and weekends, the calls went directly to her house, so sometimes I would go to her home for all night answer-prayer-line times. People often wanted to know why we would pray, and why we cared.

"I had already developed a solid prayer life at home, but here the Holy Spirit helped me see into personal situations and gave me the prayers to pray.

"When people called back, I would hear their testimonies, 'God answered! I want to know the same God you know.' I was able to lead people to the Lord as a result.

"God has always been there for me in the context of prayer, but this Pioneer Girls' leader mentored me."

Christie emphasized the importance of trust in mentorship.

"There were powerful women of prayer where I lived and I gleaned from them. This small community developed a solid core group that met together several times a week for church, worship practice, Bible studies, and prayer. I could hear the ease with which they prayed. They were confident to pray bold prayers. They often prayed the Word of God and were so sure God would take care of whatever they prayed about.

"If anything off was going on, they automatically said, 'Let's pray about it.'

"One person involved in prayer and worship broke the trust of the group. Afterward, I withdrew a lot from praying corporately. I didn't feel safe in a group anymore. It was such a big hit for us all.

"When I moved, I lost a lot of my prayer mentors. I'm still claiming back some of that space in my personal life and gradually gaining the confidence to speak and be vulnerable with a prayer group. Mentorship is so valuable and important."

Unmasking the Myth

The teaching that prayer is a private journey developed *only* in seclusion is a myth. There is an element of truth that most prayer time is intimate one-on-one time spent with God. But the myth attempts to both keep us from exponentially learning from those around us and setting an example for yet others to follow.

An old expression says, "More is caught than taught." In mentoring and modeling there is an opportunity to both catch the wind of others' prayers and to learn from their example.

We need only look at Jesus to see true disciple-making is both caught and taught. He spent three years eating, sleeping, walking, talking and living all aspects of His life with a renegade group of followers. They observed prayer at its finest.

Jesus spent most of His time alone with His disciples—mentoring and modeling everything they would need to know and do.

His disciples received the most intense form of prayer training and development. They sacrificed homes, families, businesses and personal agendas to learn from the Master.

> **"One day Jesus was praying in a certain place.**
> **When he finished, one of his disciples said to him,**
> **'Lord, teach us to pray, just as John taught**
> **his disciples.' "**
> **Luke 11:1**

Often Jesus went into solitary places to pray. The only One who heard Him was His Father (Mt 14:23, Mk 1:35; 6:46, Lk 5:16; 6:12). Whenever the disciples heard and observed Jesus in prayer, they recognized an authority, power and personal connection with the Father that they did not yet possess. They desired the same intimate closeness with the Father that Jesus experienced. Jesus taught they too could access this prayer domain.

The disciples heard the rawness of Jesus' pleas, the surrendering of His will, and the mercy and grace that infiltrated His prayers (Mt 27:46, Lk 23:34, 46). They witnessed the miraculous results of Jesus' prayers as storms ceased, abundant provision flowed, and innumerable deliverances and healings occurred.

If Jesus modeled prayer so openly to others, wisdom says we are to do likewise.

I can become comfortable in my prayer journey, feeling quite satisfied in my relationship with God. But when I witness someone else entering an intimacy with the Father I don't yet know, I'm instantly hungry for more,
more of what they have,
more of what I know I lack,
more authoritative declaration of the Word,
more boldness and confidence,
more faith and assurance in prayer,
more intimacy with the Father.
That hunger only increases as I witness others
more powerful in prayer,
receiving answers I am still pleading for,

<blockquote>
taking spiritual territory I long to possess,
and releasing God's will on Earth
as it is in Heaven.
</blockquote>

Every spring and fall, I'm enamored by the great flocks of geese passing overhead on their migration journey. I view with curiosity how first one forceful leader will move to the front and how the others follow in the path of least resistance. Then another will take the frontal position and the flock quickly adjusts to the new leader. As they travel high above vast tracts of land, this constant movement guides them to their destination.

Like these geese, the biblical leaders and prayer mentors of former generations took up their positions to lead as prayer models. Paul boldly declared,

> **"Join together in following my example, brothers**
> **and sisters, and just as you have us as a model,**
> **keep your eyes on those who live as we do."**
> **Philippians 3:17**

Here is a simple prayer asking God for prayer mentors and models,

> *"Lord, I ask You to bring people into my life who are*
> *powerful and effective in prayer. May I be teachable and*
> *pliable in prayer, learning from others. I thank You*
> *for the intimacy with You I already experience in my*
> *private prayer time. Holy Spirit, lead me into prayer*
> *encounters with others who will mentor me and*
> *model godly prayer strategies. I desire to grow*
> *and develop in prayer. Bring others who are*
> *wise and discerning in the realm of*
> *prayer into my life."*

> *"Mom and Dad held prayer meetings in our house. As a little girl, I would fall asleep kneeling surrounded by the sound of prayer."*
> — June

***

> *"Two senior church elders modeled prayer well. They made specific requests keeping their prayers real and simple—nothing flowery. They showed me prayer wasn't a 'have to do' thing."*
> — Keith

***

> *"I was never taught to pray. I listened and heard other people praying from their hearts and then I followed their example."*
> — Lois

CHAPTER 6

Daily Discipline – Rooted Habit

> *"Prayer is far less me going to God with my list and far more about going to God with a blank paper and letting Him write the blueprints."*
> *– Emmanuel*

The stirring in the tiny bed next to her signaled the beginning of another day. Sheila forced her weary body from her bed before the hunger cries of her two-month-old woke the rest of her family. As a mother of three preschool children, the necessities of others predetermined her schedule.

"No alarm clock needed these days," she thought, as she watched the rising sun transform the sky from a dusky grey to ever-changing wisps of orange and red.

Sheila's relationship with Jesus was almost as new as her youngest child. Often, she wondered why no one had told her about

Him sooner. She felt the tenacity to know God and His Word. As she sat feeding her baby, she related to his urgent need for food.

She felt the incessant cries of her soul for more of God. The longing was insatiable, even ravenous; yet daily responsibilities refused to willingly release spare moments for such selfish luxury. Time had to be seized with calculated determination.

Doing dishes at the kitchen sink became an opportunity to memorize single Bible verses or smaller portions of Scripture. During longer monotonous tasks, she did the same with entire books of the Bible. No one demanded it. No one told her it was essential to her development as a Christian.

The spiritual hunger she possessed was as natural as her baby's desire for milk. She craved God's sustaining Word—wanting it in her, available for access in every circumstance.

If this was discipline, Sheila didn't realize it. The word "discipline" held unruly connotations in her mind, like the action necessary for insubordinate behavior. That kind of discipline didn't apply to the longing of her heart. Everything about her relationship with God was nothing short of pure joy.

Similarly, no one needed to tell Sheila about the importance of prayer. Prayer, vibrant and fresh, naturally flowed throughout her day as she talked with God. Whether

laughing or crying,

sharing secrets or expressing frustration,

asking honest questions, or waiting quietly,

prayer was as essential as breathing. Prayer was the umbilical cord of this relationship between Father and daughter.

Though she had a wonderful father, there was no Father like God. She was married to a excellent husband, yet even he was incomparable to the Husband and Lover of her soul she now partnered with. Sheila was blessed with many friends, but few if any knew the deepest longings, desires, and passions she shared openly with this Friend.

From the moment she snuggled her small children into their beds, either for a nap or a good night's sleep, she felt only one urge—to spend time with God. At the kitchen table with Bible open and surrounded by a few meager study resources, she dove into the Word of God with full force. With earnest expectation, Sheila studied, knowing He was about to speak to her, reveal His character, teach her His ways, and expand her knowledge of the things of the Spirit. Hour after precious hour passed as she meditated, wrestled, absorbed and drank ever deeper from a fountain she previously had been denied.

Day by day, these simple consistent practices became a rooted habit forged deep within the once rocky soil of her heart.

Faith sprouted and grew tenaciously upward.

Joy and anticipation mingled in confident hope.

Purpose and belonging sealed her new identity.

Courage and dignity burst into being.

This season of intense seeking and learning brought transformational changes. Every day with God was like a unopened gift to be possessed and enjoyed. Every word of the Bible she believed with childlike simplicity and faith. Her ravenous appetite for more of God would not be satisfied by anything less.

Though Sheila had often viewed her late start and lack of spiritual training as a hindrance, it proved to be a blessing. The blank slate of her heart, unmarred by religious paradigms, was the perfect palette for the finger of God to etch His truth.

Sometimes others viewed her behavior as radical or extreme. To Sheila, however, it was a natural part of her infancy in the Lord. She knew without these intense times with God she could not, nor would not, survive what was ahead.

Not every stage of her life offered the luxury of such ample time in prayer, meditation, and study. However, this season would always be looked upon with a sense of gratitude for the Holy Spirit's drawing her ever deeper. These times with God formed the solid foundation upon which all other seasons would securely stand.

> *"He woos me and calls me to set aside time to be with Him." – Dawn*

Personal Perspectives

Shelly talked about her beginnings in prayer.

"I wanted to know how to hear from God, interact with Him, and have a relationship with Him. I simply asked, 'Lord, how do I pray?'"

"He answered and said, 'Pray in Jesus' Name.'"

"I would ask Him for guidance and help to make decisions. God always answered me—sometimes in incredible, always practical detail, way beyond my knowledge. He said, 'Step one, do this; step two, do that.' When I did those things, it worked out.

"Even though I was in a painful period of life, I experienced this feeling of love and hope at the same time.

> *"Every morning I would get up looking forward to spending time with Him—overwhelmed by the incredible feeling of love."*

"When the kids started coming along, I honestly even resented them waking up and interfering with my time with God. Even after twenty years, that time in the morning is still precious to me. The day just isn't right if I get up and go without spending time with God."

Keegan explains,

"It doesn't have to look a certain way. Start where you are, but don't put it off or you will put it off indefinitely. Just start praying, but keep your expectations realistic.

"If one day you want to be praying for two hours a day, don't try to start with two hours, start with five minutes. If you want to do more, you can. Prayer is a journey you build over time, with God willingly walking with you. Don't overcomplicate it. Speak to God like you're having a conversation with anyone else.

"I have had seasons where I was spiritually lazy and life steam-rolled me. I thought, 'I will pray later.' Later, I would sluff God off again with, 'God, You know what is going on,' and then I would fall asleep. The only person I was hurting was myself. Life was so much harder when I didn't meet with Him.

"To get out of that pattern, I had to be purposeful. I set aside a time when I wouldn't be interrupted.

"Before that, I had so much fear of the unknown, but once I started consistently tapping into God as my Source, I found the peace I was looking for."

Emmanuel created a rooted habit, little by little.

"About three years ago, the Lord asked me to pray for one hour a day. I could barely pray for ten minutes! After I started praying for an hour, I wanted more time to be with Him. I have seen a lot of growth in my life by obeying God in minor things.

"We underestimate the habit of little things. Those little things set us on either a good or bad track. Designating an hour every day with God seems small, but has helped me on my prayer journey.

> *"It is the little things that build a habit."*

"Today, time in prayer has become a habit. It feels uncomfortable when I don't pray for an hour a day. I'm trying to turn my prayer time into partnering with the Lord instead of complaining, venting or going through a checklist.

"When I spend time with the Lord,
    if I pray, great!
        If I worship, great!
            If I read the Bible, great!
                If I soak in His Presence, great!
"Instead of thirty minutes of this and thirty minutes of that, I've dropped my schedule."

Merodee sees prayer as the progress of three distinct phases: childlikeness, discipline and a lifestyle of prayer.

"There is the chaos of childhood, praying as needed or as a response to circumstances. Then there is the disciplinary prayer which brings order. That's when prayer isn't flowing freely yet, but there is an intention to put structures in place. Finally, the result of the disciplined effort is the continuum of a lifestyle of prayer.

"When Holy Spirit called me into the season of discipline, I felt there was something not quite right about praying that way. Initially, it somehow felt hypocritical, but it isn't. It is important to not throw out the discipline of prayer because it's a type of training.

"We discipline ourselves to respond in a continual place of prayer, not just praying when we feel like it. Even though I didn't understand it, the more I practiced discipline, the more and more it became freeing.

"The discipline of prayer can feel awkward, even messy."

"One night at a prayer meeting a woman challenged me to pray in the Spirit for twenty minutes a day. I wanted prayer to flow effortlessly, like a babbling brook.

"I started getting up at six o'clock in the morning, not because I was disciplined, but because I felt uncomfortable and didn't want anyone to hear me. Twenty minutes seemed so long. I would pray and think, 'That has to be twenty minutes. It was only three!'

"I constantly rerouted my thoughts back to God while in my quiet place with Him. Everyday things like what I should make for lunch would pop into my mind. Playing worship music or walking around while I prayed helped me to focus.

"For the first two or three years, my early morning prayer time was only praying in the Spirit for a minimum of twenty minutes. I learned that praying that way wasn't secondary, but primary. Praying in the Spirit exercised my faith, aligning me with God. Eventually, praying in the Spirit became freeing as I spent time with Him."

The childlike wonder of being in a relationship with the Lord need never dissipate or lose the essence of the miraculous. Yet, in every believer, there is a shift in development out of childhood into maturity. Eventually, we begin to sense a personal responsibility for keeping relationship vibrant and fresh.

This purposeful development is called spiritual discipline. For an athlete training for competition, a student studying for exams, or an employee working toward a certification, an effort is required. Everyone I interviewed recognized a positive shift in their relationship with God when they took the privilege of knowing Him with a greater sense of ownership.

This ownership doesn't come out of obligation, but rather a continuation of God drawing us into deeper fellowship. When we respond, He satisfies.

> *"Prayer changed when I realized it isn't a have to rule, but a ncessary thing. It comes from the heart and not from the head." – Keith*

Caran says,

"When I don't have words to say, I know it's okay. I don't need to come anymore with a list of people I will pray for like it is my duty. Prayer has gone from responsibility to a relationship. I want to sit at His feet like Mary and hear Him speak to me and feel His love wash over me (Lk 10:39).

"We cannot feel the things Jesus feels for us if we don't sit and listen to Him. When I listen, being silent and waiting, expecting I will receive from Him in some way, I feel how much God loves me and cares about the things on my heart.

"There are many ways we can pause from our everyday life and take time to be present with Him, recognizing who He is, and that He is with us. There is a deep peace in His Presence, whether it is

    reading the Bible,
        sitting in my place of prayer,
            walking in nature,
                laying on the beach,
                    or fishing in the boat.

"If we take time to pause, being open, receiving from Him whether through a word, an image or a spiritual hug, He will give us what we need at that moment.

"The beauty is that it doesn't have to be in our prayer closet.

106

Often when I sit down at my desk to write, I will ask, 'What do You have for me today? How do You want to speak? How can I use my gift to bring glory to You and edify You?'

"When I'm driving the kids around or picking them up, it is prayer time. Sometimes prayer is silent, sometimes it is speaking out loud, 'How can I and my family serve You today?'

"You can be intentional and develop that habit of praying wherever you are. It doesn't have to be morning devotions where you kneel and pray. Take prayer with you! It isn't healthy to pray once a day and then leave God behind.

"Prayer is a lifestyle. I want to take time at each moment of my day to talk to God and to listen to Him. I don't always remember, but I am daily cultivating prayer as a lifestyle."

Isaac deliberately schedules time with God.

"I want nothing I do to be apart from God. Because it takes time, I find it beneficial to set a time for prayer. I love to get up early in the morning to pray and then pray again late at night. I schedule an appointment and say, 'God, at four o'clock, I want to meet with You.'

> "*I make appointments with God to set aside time for Him alone.*"

"I know He is always with us and knows we have busy schedules. I find it encouraging that God wants to hear from us. He wants us to ask Him to meet our needs: **'You do not have because you do not ask God'** (Jas 4:2-3).

"He is all-knowing and **'able to do exceedingly abundantly above all that we ask and think'** (Eph 3:20 KJV). For a long time that wasn't real to me. Since I started setting up appointments with God, I have seen so much fruit in my life.

"Until December last year, I wasn't working full time, so I had lots of free time. Now I have a full schedule; I need to set time apart for Him alone; I *need* that time with God. The Bible says, **'Be still, and know that I am God'** (Ps 46:10). Putting that verse into practice has changed my prayer life.

"Often when I pray, my thoughts are all over the place. When I am still, I reflect on the fact that He is God. I will thank Him for His Presence and invite Holy Spirit to come. I let Him drop things into my heart and allow the cares of this world to take the back seat for a while.

"When I don't take prayer time, my thoughts are too busy. I can quickly fall into the old habit of just sending up requests. In the stillness, He reveals Himself. Prayer centers on knowing He is God Almighty, able to do anything—even more than we could ask. It's a good thing to solidify in our hearts who He is before we pray.

"I want everyone to grow in how to be still and wait upon the Lord."

In Mongolia, where Pearl comes from, discipline is highly stressed in the Christian walk.

"At Bible school, they required us to pray for one hour in the Spirit so loud that we lost our voices. In the afternoon, we would pray for another full hour the same way. We also studied the Bible and were taught how to minister to others.

"They told us, 'Pray! Pray! Pray!'

"Bible school helped form the foundation of my prayer life. I only prayed a short time in my language but in the prayer language at least an hour.

"When I left Bible school and began working, I disciplined myself to continue praying for one hour in the morning and then another hour after work. We tend to pray when we need God, but I didn't want that. I would kneel and pray no matter how I felt.

> *"When I pray, I feel God's peace and receive strength."*

"God started speaking to me through Bible verses, often directing me to a specific reference. More and more consistently, I heard Him."

At times, the discipline of prayer may feel like work, but it is work without labor. Charlene is a wife, mother and business owner who has learned to juggle her time to make room for God.

"I want to learn all about Jesus. When I came to Christ just a couple of years ago, I knew nothing. My Mom had given me a Bible ten years prior, but it sat in my closet. After I began my relationship with Christ, I opened my Bible and thought, 'I don't know how to read this thing.'

"Now I wake up at six o'clock to have time with God. I go to my room, close the door and sing to Him for about an hour in praise and worship. Sometimes the Presence of God will become especially known. I give Him thanks and say, 'I'm here to listen. What do You want to tell me today?'

> *"Sometimes I don't want to leave the room because God's Presence is so strong."*

"He will say, 'Okay, your time is up; have a great day. You need to feed your kids.' Not that I can't talk with Him all day long, but that time in the morning is so wonderful and peaceful it is honestly hard to leave.

"I engaged in whatever opportunity came my way to help me grow spiritually, including prayer nights, Holy Spirit nights, discipleship classes and Master's Commission. I have mentors who encourage me to keep pressing in during my times alone with God. They help me keep the hunger for more of Him.

> *"There will always be more of God to experience."*

"I know God is real. Every day I want to be in His Presence and to know His heart. It's a daily part of my life to want to press into Him and seek the Kingdom of God."

Kate says simply,

"I was always seeking a closer relationship with God. The Lord was wooing, loving and drawing me unto Himself.

"Just like Jesus and the Father are one, we are one with Him. **'For in Him we live and move and have our being'** (Jn 10:30, Acts 17:28). As we become more comfortable in our relationship with Him and our revelation of Him, we walk in that oneness to a greater and greater degree."

Unmasking the Myth

There is a myth fostering apathetic indifference toward the discipline of prayer. It's the belief that prayer is best left to the responsibility of pastors, ministers or other professionals. We assume these trained experts are more effective in prayer.

Nothing could be farther from the truth. In Matthew 6:5, Jesus said to His disciples, **"When you pray . . ."** He didn't say, *"if"* you pray, but *"when."* It was a foregone conclusion that everyone should and would be actively praying.

> **". . . The prayer of a righteous person is**
> **powerful and effective."**
> **James 5:16b**

Prayer is like a spiritual muscle—a skill to be developed. It takes time and practice. The experiences of these men and women remind us to start small, beginning with *the little things*, until prayer becomes a rooted habit. Private times with God allow us to be *real* in our growing process.

> *"Significant suddenlies happen*
> *when we have set structures in our lives."*
> *— Pastor Rob Reimer*

As we establish the discipline of prayer, we discover God is beyond the limitations of time or space. Then we can understand the continuity of past, present, and future with greater clarity. The rooted habit of prayer equips us to
>live authentically today,
>>possess God's promises for the future,
>>>center around His eternal perspectives,
>>>>courageously stand through trials,
>>>live peacefully in a confused world
>>and display Christ to those around us.

Let's not leave to the so-called professionals what God has intended for us all to enjoy. Let's crush the myth that would keep us from the most significant time available—time with God. We can begin where we are and take prayer one notch farther.

Some helpful tips:

1. Make an appointment with God by establishing a set time.

2. Decide on a convenient time and place to meet with Him.
3. To minimize interruptions, keep a box of essential supplies, like a Bible, a journal, and a writing tool near your quiet place of prayer.
4. If it isn't too distracting, play instrumental worship music to help your mind focus.

Experiment to find the time of day when you are the most alert, and the least distracted. It might be a struggle to establish the discipline aspect of prayer, but consistency pays off. Sometimes, you too might question, "Is this prayer?" As you persist, you will soon look forward to this personal time spent with God. Once you commit yourself to create the rooted habit of prayer, you will reap the rewards of your efforts.

> **"And pray in the Spirit on all occasions with all
> kinds of prayers and requests. With this in mind,
> be alert and always keep on praying for
> all the Lord's people."**
> **Ephesians 6:18**

I use the acronym **"S-T-E-P"** to guide my quiet time with God.

S – Start by reading a portion of *Scripture*. It isn't how much or how little you read, but rather the consistency of reading the Bible. Many daily reading plans and devotionals are available to help you.

T – Stands for *takeaway*. What is God speaking to you through this passage? Questions to ask might be:
- What application can I pull from these verses?
- What does this teach me about God's character?
- Is there an action point or area of growth for me to pursue?
- How does this relate to my circumstances or relationships?

E – The best time for most people is *early* in the day, giving God first place before clutter, activity or an overload of responsibilities demand attention.

P – *Prayer* is an integral part of our time with God. Prayer may include:
- coming into agreement with God's Word
- committing to follow Him
- thanksgiving and praise for who He is or what He has done

- presenting the needs of others
- making personal requests
- waiting silently in His Presence

Here is one more word of encouragement.

> **"So then, just as you received Christ Jesus as
> Lord, continue to live your lives in him,
> *rooted and built up* in him, strengthened in
> the faith as you were taught, and
> overflowing with thankfulness."**
> **Colossians 2:6-7**
> (Emphasis mine)

Before long, you will have enough incentive and momentum to keep on going. Just a few simple steps will lead to a habit of prayer. Soon, you will be eager to share with others the multiple answers to prayer you are encountering.

> *"Father, thank You for Your open invitation to spend
> time with You. I approach the discipline of prayer
> with excitement and trepidation, sensing what a priv-
> ilege it is. I know with discipline it isn't the thought
> that counts, but a necessary action. Help me, Lord, to
> move past any roadblocks to progress in prayer through
> consistently placing You first. God, I desire to become
> rooted and built up in You, so I ask You to meet
> me as I come boldly into Your presence . . ."*

> *"God has pursued me to make time for him early in the
> morning. Jesus and Dawn every day! He will wake
> me early. In the last eight years, it has stuck."*
> *– Dawn*

***

> "Prayer is a practiced discipline. I always start my morning with the Lord—loving Him, pouring my heart out to Him, along with studying and reading the Word."
> – Karli

***

> "It is never too late to start praying!"
> – June

CHAPTER 7

Hunger & Thirst
– Oasis of Prayer

> *"Prayer became my food. I prayed like I was a ravenous*
> *woman. I hungered for His Presence."*
> *– Helen*

Like a baby forced from the muted surroundings of a cushioned womb, my spiritual birth thrust me into a previously unknown way of life. Everything about a personal relationship with Jesus was unfamiliar. One thing was for sure, the taste of prayer and communion with God was sweet and satisfying to my parched soul.

For the first time, I began to delve into a depth of love and freedom that remains undefinable. In this new life with Christ, I felt an unlimited ability to

      stretch and reach,

            experience and explore,

                  discover and develop,

                      grow and achieve,

                            build and establish.

How could a simple prayer of dedicating one's life to Jesus Christ make so much difference? My single-minded focus on self-sufficiency was toppled. Multi-directional connections with God and others brought both inward and outward satisfaction.

That first taste of prayer ignited an insatiable appetite for the divine. Each encounter with God intensified my hunger for more. The most profound encounters with God could not permanently satiate such a desire for more. The Bible opened another door to an ever-expanding realm of the impossible made possible.

From the beginning of my prayer journey, I craved
> to know Him more completely,
>> to be with Him more intimately,
>>> to hear Him more succinctly,
> to see Him more clearly,
>> to understand Him more fully,
>>> to engage with Him more deeply.

Is this ravenous appetite for more of God's Presence prayer? Is such craving a sign of something gone wrong, or something that's unquestionably right?

Have you heard the wails of a newborn baby thirsty for milk? Only one thing can silence its desperate pleas or quiet its gnawing need—the sweet milk of its mother.

The voracious appetite for God, to meet Him in prayer, is a sure sign of a healthy, growing believer. It is a lack of appetite that symbolizes dis-ease.

Thankfully, the gluttonous desire for more of God has never subsided. Throughout decades of walking with God, the validity of such hunger has been proven time and time again. Often, the only One I had to cling to was God and the only thing able to sustain me was prayer. He has always been enough!

It is this constant hunger for the Presence of God through prayer that has carried me through the
> brokenness of relationships,
>> loss and sorrows of the heart,
>>> bouts of depression and anxiety,
>>>> serious illness and disease,
>>>>> struggles and trials.

Hunger is a God gift. It is a grace gift awakening every believer to a need that would otherwise go unnoticed and unmet. I am not alone in this hungry pursuit of God or thirst for His Presence.

> *"The church is being moved to an awakening hunger for God." – Candice*

Personal Perspectives

Helen relates to this ever-deepening desire for God.

"Even as a child of ten or eleven years old, I wanted to serve God, but I knew I wasn't. Every night before I went to bed, I would lift my hand and say, 'God don't let me get away.' I did not understand who God was, yet this was my prayer almost every night.

"Over the years, I did the religious stuff of reading my Bible and going to church. However, I never had a conscious awareness of Him. I was thirty-six years old when I came to the Lord. Immediately, I sought Him through Bible reading and prayer. My food was to be in the Presence of God interceding in prayer. I prayed like a ravenous woman!

"At that time, I had Chronic Fatigue Syndrome. As soon as my husband left for work, I would go into my quiet place, remaining there for hours. I didn't even care if I was sick. I often sat in God's Presence without even praying, and I experienced healing both in body and soul.

"The Bible says God makes me lie down, and He restores my soul (Ps 23:3 NKJV). In the place of quietness and rest, prayer and waiting, He restored me. Words weren't necessary.

> *"Prayer developed out of a deep hunger for God."*

"My husband and I have often driven for miles without talking, but we know we are loved and valued. When you're with your spouse or a best friend, you don't have to talk all the time to feel the love between you. I feel the same way with God. Prayer is simply being with the Lord and communicating with Him. I don't think it has to include words all the time.

"God is so big! How could we even dare to describe God? Oh, the depth of the wisdom and knowledge of God. His ways are beyond finding out. There is so much more to God than we know. No man has seen God, but we will see Him and be like Him (Jn 1:18, 1 Jn 3:2).

"I have been asking God to turn me away from possessions. I have many nice things, nice clothes, and nice jewelry. But in the face of God, I want to keep everything at arm's length, desiring only Him."

God is beyond comparison. Everything becomes shallow in the light of His Presence. Emily shared,

"Prayer is one of my favorite things, never a burden. There have been both small and big steps in my prayer journey to bring me to where I am now.

"A small step happened when I was nineteen years old while working at a summer camp. Another girl and I became friends. We both wanted to stay deeply connected to God and to overcome the awkwardness of praying out loud. We broke silent prayer by praying together as we went about the day praying over the horses and campers, and while doing chores or walking around the grounds.

"That summer, there were things about Holy Spirit I didn't understand but I was hungry for. I had friends who prayed in tongues, and I wanted to figure this out. Four boys at camp came from the same family. At every opportunity, I drilled them with questions about the Holy Spirit and speaking in tongues. When I went on a road trip with their mom, I questioned her more. She was such a loving woman and explained everything to me. Later, I asked her and her husband, along with other leaders at the camp, to pray for me so I could be baptized in the Holy Spirit and receive my prayer language of tongues.

"It was another enormous step for me in my prayer journey when I became connected to a house of prayer. For a long time, I had been hungry for fellowship with other people of prayer. I realized prayer was a part of who I am; I instantly fit with others who lived the life of prayer. Pastor Graham kept saying, 'Prayer is not what we do; it is who we are.' It is a part of our relationship with God, so I can't leave it behind.

"Everything about my life and faith grew around other people who prayed intentionally and passionately. My hunger for more of God and prayer increased so much."

Keegan said,

"Until my early adult years, I saw God as angry or stoic. I understood He wanted a relationship with us, but I believed it came with stipulations. I knew God heard, but I had thought when we did something wrong there were consequences. It took me a while to realize the grace of God.

"Knowing you have the ear of the Alpha and Omega is not something you ever fully comprehend. I began to understand prayer is not just a cute little memorization before bedtime, but a continual dialogue with God.

> *"Prayer is not polished language but honestly speaking what we are feeling to God."*

"One of my leaders at a ministry boot camp was in charge of the house I stayed in. He would get up early to pray for his team and would gather the guys together to pray. I worked with him on different ministry groups. After watching his example, conversations about prayer opened up between us.

"I never had formal training but praying with those leaders changed my life. I would ask them questions about the role prayer had in their lives. Their passion for prayer increased hunger and desire for the rest of us. Seeing how they prayed, and what they prayed for, stirred up my prayers and helped me to detach from other things. Their impact was both visible and verbal.

"We were on fire for God and wanted to see God move. We had a hunger to pursue God more."

Karli shared,

"Prayer has become an ongoing thing in my life. I speak to God and hear from Him throughout the day, never turning prayer off. Some people might even call me crazy or too intense, but I want to foster a continuous posture of speaking to and hearing from God in every detail of life.

> *"God is a God of mystery—press in and hunger."*

"God says, **'Blessed are those who hunger and thirst . . . for they will be filled'** (Mt 5:6). I never want to limit God, so I press into Him and hunger for more. I want to catch whatever

He is saying or doing. In prayer, I am rolling on the waves and frequencies of Heaven. I want to ride those waves all the way.

"I hunger and thirst for God, jumping up to Daddy, singing, praising and seeing Heaven come down to Earth."

Charlene agrees,

"Whatever God has for me, I want. After about an hour of worshiping God and waiting in His Presence, I felt Holy Spirit right there with me.

"At first, I tried to figure out how? Now I know, I don't need to figure out how. I have no idea how! God is so big, so much bigger than I think.

"There are no words for Him, for His power and glory. He is so loving. There was never a time I was afraid of God, although I've had other fears that have tried to keep me from going *to* God. Whenever I have pushed through my fear, God has shown Himself amazing.

"My hunger and thirst for God grow with the revelation of how big and real He is. That He is in me, working things out in my life, never grows dull."

Caran also experiences deep spiritual hunger and thirst.

"Before, my relationship with Jesus was more like going on a dating app. I would put myself out there telling Him, 'These are my characteristics and needs.' I would do the same with Him, evaluating and checking Him out, clicking and liking the things I wanted, without taking the time to meet with Him or get to know Him better. My relationship was more of a one-way thing.

"When I became a Christian, I remember feeling such a hunger for Him. I would turn on my praise music and just lie on the floor weeping. I deeply wanted the nearness of Jesus to come. I had this hunger for God, but I didn't realize I could tell Him about it.

"As my relationship with Jesus developed, I wanted to know Him more and listen to Him. I still have days when I am so hungry for Him."

Through fellowship with other believers, Isaac developed a hunger to see God move in the lives of others.

"When I first dedicated my life to Jesus, I would go to church and then back home, but I was disconnected from the Christian community. However, when I started to meet with people who were active in their pursuit of God, it changed my perspective.

"I saw others my age out on the streets praying for strangers. When I started seeing healings and salvations, I was hungry to see more of that in my life. I wanted to be praying for people too, leading them to Jesus and seeing God heal them.

"Fellowship with other Christians who were active in their faith drew me into evangelism, boldly praying for people. It created a hunger in me to see God move more. That's when things changed in my prayer life. Over and over, God has shown me how real He is."

An intense hunger for both God and prayer accentuates Merodee's life.

"There was no arrogance when Paul told the church to imitate him. We are supposed to imitate things we see in others until it becomes our own. For a long time, I believed imitating others in prayer was ineffective, but in the body of Christ, we share our testimony. Your testimony is powerful in my life and becomes fuel for my prayers. Testimony intensifies hunger in others.

> *"A culture of prayer becomes a culture of testimony."*

"We aren't to covet other people's prayer life or prayer styles, because coveting will rob us. However, by listening and watching others, we can increase our hunger and passion for prayer.

"There is a young man in our church who has dedicated himself to prayer. Now he is enjoying the fruit of the lifestyle of prayer. When he prays, the only thing I want to do is kneel and worship God. When I look at his life, I ask, 'What You have done in his life Lord, do it again.'"

Sharon said,

"Shortly after I accepted Christ, I was alone in my living room one night when Jesus came and stood in front of me. I didn't see Him, but I heard Him—not audibly but in my spirit, speaking Isaiah 61 to me,

> 'The Spirit of the Sovereign LORD is on me,
> because the LORD has anointed me
> to proclaim good news to the poor.
> He has sent me to bind up the brokenhearted,

123

> to proclaim freedom for the captives
> and release from darkness for the prisoners,
> to proclaim the year of the LORD's favor
> and the day of vengeance of our God,
> to comfort all who mourn, and provide for those
> who grieve in Zion — to bestow on them a crown
> of beauty instead of ashes, the oil of joy instead of
> mourning and a garment of praise instead
> of a spirit of despair . . .'
> **Isaiah 61:1-3**

"The way His Presence came out of nowhere blew me away. There was no question in my mind it was Jesus. When you hear His voice, there's no doubt it is Him. The combination of experiencing His Presence, and the desperation I felt for His help, filled me with a hunger for prayer.

"Desperation! Tough place to be, but a good place to be."

"I had three boys to raise, and I knew I wasn't equipped for parenting. I honestly didn't know how to mother well. I had read about someone laying prostrate in the Presence of the Lord, so I stayed up late at night or got up in the middle of the night to pray. There, all alone, I was determined to lie before God, seeking His Kingdom and His righteousness (Mt 6:33).

"In that place of desperation and hunger, prayer was birthed in me. I had read about people who would worship the Lord for an hour or two each day. I hungered and prayed for that kind of heart. God answered and gave me both a seeking heart and a worshiping spirit. It wasn't something I worked at. It was easy.

"Nobody ever sat down and explained to me how to pray or how not to pray. Prayer came from what God did in me."

"The Lord allows us to go through desperate times to bring us to our faces, hungry and desperate enough to do business with Him."

Unmasking the Myth

What myth lies beneath hunger or lack of it? It's the myth that falsely warns about the danger of being "so heavenly minded you become no earthly good."

The insinuation is that by spending too much time with God, you will be useless everywhere else. Those who believe this lie also believe balance is the ultimate solution. Truthfully, if we place equal importance on everything, then nothing is ever more important. The myth of balance declares moderation as preeminent.

Even a quick search of Scripture at the life of Jesus challenges the point. Jesus forewarned His disciples that to follow Him meant

giving up everything,

taking up a cross daily,

sacrificing home, family and security,

seeking His Kingdom over and above all, and

possessing a willingness to be misunderstood, maligned or even martyred.

I find it hard to discover balanced mediocrity in either Jesus' life or His teachings. He possessed a single-minded pursuit to do all He saw His Father doing and to speak all He heard His Father speak. He gave everything for us.

Jesus' love propelled Him beyond any preconceived paradigm of balanced tradition or religion. His radical love led Him to the cross to reconcile all of humanity to Himself.

C. S. Lewis said, "If you read history you will find that the Christians who did most for the present world were just those who thought most of the next. The Apostles themselves, who set on foot the conversion of the Roman Empire, the great men who built up the Middle Ages, the English Evangelicals who abolished the Slave Trade, all left their mark on Earth, precisely because their minds were occupied with Heaven. It is since Christians have largely ceased to think of the other world that they have become so ineffective in this one. Aim at Heaven and you will get Earth 'thrown in'; aim at Earth and you will get neither."[1]

The fear of becoming too radical for Jesus might be the very thing keeping us from entering the fullness of what we inwardly crave.

Though I have never experienced famine in the natural sense, I have willingly fasted for periods. The longer the fast, the less hungry I became for food. Sometimes it took even longer to reintroduce food than the time the fast lasted. In the absence of this nourishment, my body forgot how desperate the need was.

There's a spiritual equivalent. We can be apart from God for so long we lose comprehension of how critical prayer and Bible reading are to the soul. Even though spiritual hunger cannot be articulated at that point in our lives, it demands to be pacified even if by lesser things.

Can spiritual hunger and thirst be fostered? When someone has been *starved* of the Presence of God, will hunger awaken again?

Yes, it will! If you wait until you have it all figured out, it might be too late. Start where you are and go from there. Be careful not to set unrealistic expectations for yourself. Ask God for an increased hunger to know Him and the things of His Kingdom.

> **"For the eyes of the LORD range throughout the**
> **earth to strengthen those whose hearts**
> **are fully committed to him . . ."**
> **2 Chronicles 16:9**

As soon as God sees the desire for increased hunger, He will partner with even our smallest efforts. He invites, **"Open wide your mouth and I will fill it"** (Ps 81:10).

> *"We need to become dependent so much on God there is no Plan B. When we have that kind of hunger and desperation, waiting for only Him to speak, He will show up!"* – Perry

I wonder how many times we turn away from God's offer to satisfy our spiritual needs because we neither know nor trust Him. Yet, He continually welcomes us to come to eat and drink of His Presence.

> **"Come, all you who are thirsty, come to the waters;**
> **and you who have no money, come, buy and eat!**
> **Come, buy wine and milk without**
> **money without cost."**
> **Isaiah 55:1**

The more we know God, the more of God we want to know. The more we nurture a hunger and thirst for Him, the more that hunger intensifies within us.

A baby starts off drinking only milk in tiny quantities. As the child grows, the need for nourishment naturally increases both in quantity and substance. Soon milk is not enough; the craving for solid food intensifies.

> *"You need to knock, keep knocking and keep knocking! You may not hear Him immediately but don't quit." – Heather*

Hunger is a natural part of physical and spiritual health. When hunger is absent in our physical bodies, it is usually a sign of illness or disease. I often ask God to reveal anything that might hinder my hunger and thirst for Him. Various disorders can block what should be a natural craving for more of His Presence:

unforgiveness or bitterness,
critical judgments of others,
pride or refusal to acknowledge need,
busyness and preoccupation with lesser things,
trying to satisfy spiritual hunger

through natural means, materialism or addictions. Temporary things numb but never satisfy the longing for God's Presence.

> **"You, God, are my God, earnestly I seek you;**
> **I thirst for you, my whole being longs for you,**
> **in a dry and parched land where there is no water."**
> **Psalm 63:1**

There was a time when the going became tough, and everyone

was deserting Jesus. But Peter said, **"Lord, to whom shall we go? You have the words of eternal life"** (Jn 6:68). Peter may not have always had his facts straight, his disciple coat on right-side-out, or his sandals pointing in the right direction, but this time, he understood. In Christ alone is life; only God satisfies.

> *"Lord I confess I don't always hunger for You like I should. Create in me an increased hunger and thirst that will turn me wholeheartedly to You. You are the Source for everything life-giving. As You cause me to hunger and thirst, allow me also to experience the joy of being fully satisfied in Your Presence."*

> *"I am seeing the hunger for prayer and worship take down denominational lines."*
> *— Candice*

***

> *"Are we desperate enough and determined enough to work with God to see God move."*
> *— Sharon*

***

> *"Don't settle for the old; you have tasted the new."*
> *— Merodee*

***

Notes
1. C. S. Lewis, Mere Christianity, 66. https://www.dacc.edu/assets/pdfs/PCM/merechristianitylewis.pdf

CHAPTER 8

Prayer Journals
– Ears to Hear

> *"I journal, writing all my thoughts and leaving*
> *them on the page to get all the chaos out.*
> *Then I can be quiet, wait and pray."*
> *– Christie*

"I barely remember a time," said Nathan, "when the haze of depression didn't drag my movements to near-stagnation."

Both Nathan's father and mother experienced extended bouts of mental illness. His father would withdraw in quiet solitude, unable to relate to his son in a way his young heart craved. His mother's episodes of uncontrollable rage created deep and long-lasting bruises.

Nathan was uncertain how young he was when he first stole shots of alcohol from his father's liquor cabinet. In his mid-teens, already a bona fide alcoholic, only the desire for death outweighed his addiction. Hospitalization was neither the beginning nor the end of his life-threatening battle with mental illness.

It was in this season that Nathan was introduced to the Serenity

Prayer—penned on a scrap piece of notepaper, given unceremoniously.

> *"God grant me the serenity to accept the things I cannot*
> *change, courage to change the things I can and wisdom*
> *to know the difference."* [1]

Instinctively, Nathan knew something significant in this brief prayer held the key to his survival. Just how, he was uncertain. As far as he was concerned, God was unknown, non-existent, or at the very least, far removed. If serenity, courage, and wisdom could be found, Nathan didn't know where.

At times, waves of darkness threatened to engulf him whole. Tormenting thoughts swept over him with tsunami force wiping away all normalcy. Try as he might to maintain equilibrium, the dark ebbs struck with relentless inconsistency, sapping all strength and desire to live.

Oddly enough, a couple of years later a drinking buddy randomly gave Nathan a Dollar Store version of the Serenity Prayer. Nathan threw it into a drawer, quickly forgetting its haunting message. The words hung like scented mist, faintly visible wafts of hope, filtered almost imperceptibly through the hardened crust of his heart.

Sometime later, a colleague from work emailed Nathan the full version, sensing he needed encouragement. Nathan briefly mused over the phrases. He printed them out before pushing the delete button.

> *"Living one day at a time; enjoying one moment at*
> *a time; accepting hardships as the pathway to peace;*
> *taking, as Jesus did, this sinful world as it is, not as I*
> *would have it; trusting He will make all things right if*
> *I surrender to His Will; that I may be reasonably*
> *happy in this life and supremely happy with*
> *Him forever in the next."*

Neither the author, Reinhold Niebuhr, nor Nathan's co-worker knew the depth of his "one day at a time" struggle or how impossible it was to "enjoy one moment at a time."

Nathan's life was marked by his rough habits, terrible choices, and irresponsible attitudes. Taking an honest look at his own self-made "sinful world" wasn't easy. As far as he was concerned, even God couldn't "make all things right."

Nevertheless, the Serenity Prayer gave Nathan a nail-hold on sanity, a *by-the-skin-of-his-teeth* ability to endure just one more day. Perhaps tomorrow the light would break through his impenetrable darkness.

Two decades after his first hospitalization, Nathan was convinced death was his only reprieve. He left home one day, with full intentions of never returning. He would make one stop for a few items before ending his years of torment. When Nathan entered the hardware store, the first thing he noticed was a plaque with the Serenity Prayer. Turning on his heels, he walked out of the store empty-handed and emotionally numb.

The now-familiar words of the prayer uncapped an artesian well of buried emotion. God's sovereign love and care tangibly engulfed him. Nathan sat weeping in his car for a long time before turning the ignition and returning home. Even amidst hopelessness and helplessness, he knew somehow, someway, his darkest days were over.

The Bible and spontaneous prayer anchored Nathan. However, it was this little written prayer, a prayer penned over a century before which

gave hope in the absence of hope,

offered peace to his tormented mind,

brought comfort to his hard existence,

deposited courage in his fear-filled heart,

and strengthened Nathan to hold on. The Serenity Prayer helped Nathan to realize **"when I am weak, then I am strong"** (2 Cor 12:10).

Nathan adds, "I live free from depression and mental illness today, thanks to the intervention of many trained and untrained mentors, counselors, friends, and family. I am thankful God never let go of me, even when I was more than ready to throw in the towel and quit life forever. A written prayer didn't save me from my self-destructive thoughts and behaviors, God did. However, the Serenity Prayer consistently caused me to rethink the existence of God at critical moments in my life."

Nathan wasn't the only one who mentioned the power of written prayers. Many faiths use written prayers as a consistent and reliable means of conveying heartfelt desires and petitions. Some people preferred to write their prayers to pass on to others or to use personally. Others disregarded the potential of written prayers.

The spiritual practice of journaling includes recording prayers, challenges and insights God is teaching us. In a broad sense, we might even view the Bible as a God-breathed journal, written through the hands of many Holy Spirit inspired writers.

Can you hear the disciples later discussing the many things Jesus spoke and taught? What important lessons and prayers should they record that would be strategic to coming generations of believers? Can you hear them wrestle with what to include and what to leave out of their journal of the life and times of Jesus Christ? Some of

their blunders were downright embarrassing,

their insights when spiritually discerned amazing,

their water walking faith awe-inspiring,

their frail humanity encouraging,

their weak-willed dedication appalling,

their natural instincts of self-promotion humbling,

their devotion worthy of applauding.

They wrote it all to us!

Many people have found penning words to paper beneficial in their pursuit of prayer. Writing prayers, meditations, or God lessons can take a variety of forms.

Personal Perspectives

Merodee struggled with the authenticity of written prayers.

"I felt condemned for praying someone else's written prayers and thought they were less fruitful, especially for my marriage. When my husband and I started leading a couple's group, we suggested they pray using books like Stormie Omartian's *The Power of the Praying Wife, The Power of the Praying Husband* or

The Power of a Praying Parent.

"We started praying for each other and our children this way too. We learned written prayers are not secondary. They create a foundation for us of the rhythm and flow of prayer from which our prayers can branch out. Whereas before, we felt uncomfortable praying for each other, now prayer became sweet and innocent.

"The Apostle Paul said, **'Follow my example, as I follow the example of Christ'** (1 Cor 11:1)."

Most of Patrick's writing takes the form of written prayers.

"I don't generally journal, although, I've been journaling since I went on missions and am in ministry training. I have written out prayers. It gave me time to think deeply about what the words mean, what I was trying to pray for, and to get a solid foundation of what I'm trying to pray out. When I write a prayer out, I think about the words I am using and gain a greater understanding of how I am praying.

"I also kept a written prayer in my wallet, pulling it out and praying it sometimes.

"There was a specific time when I sent out a prayer by email that was thoughtfully written. I took a long time formulating the words and what they meant. As soon as I hit send, that prayer was fulfilled."

Praying and writing join in perfect unison the communication movements with and of God. The rhythm of prayer changes dramatically—sometimes slow and pensive, other times prophetic and exhilarating, then introspective or travailing.

The term "journaling" can sound demanding and rigid. It's astonishing the diversity writing can take when joined with the language of prayer. Free-flow writing is perhaps one unexpected form.

Dawn finds through writing she can hear God's voice more clearly and can also formulate a response to His promptings.

"God speaks to me through inaudible words or statements in my mind and spirit. I know when it's Him. Sometimes God speaks while I'm writing. The Holy Spirit will lead me to get my journal and just write. It will be a word I don't hear until I begin to write.

"Recently in my writing, I heard one little statement, 'Master the menial.' God's voice is never condemning, but instructive.

> *"When I talk to God, He is always present.*
> *He has always been present."*

"One day, I was upset with both myself and my husband. The next morning, I made my little *nest* on the floor with a blanket, my Bible, journal, and coffee. I started to journal, telling the Lord how upset I was feeling.

"I felt led to write down my shortcomings, like impatience, anger when I don't get my way, uncontrolled tongue, words of strife, and negative attitudes. I knew immediately as I was writing God was showing me the error of my ways. I repented of each one. I focused on impatience and to see what impatience had cost me.

"God is so loving! He doesn't say, 'Don't do that!' He lovingly leads us."

For many people, journaling is a way to record their dialogue with God to access later.

My own experiences of writing my conversations with God were probably more painful than they needed to be. Journaling started more like a diary in which I poured out my thoughts and emotions to God. Often, I would tear up or burn the pages later, unwilling for others to read the depth of my angst.

Eventually, I found the habit of writing my thoughts and recording any God impressions amazingly insightful. I would often write far more than my mind was capable of thinking on its own.

> *"Sometimes it's like someone has downloaded an entire program—a new area of understanding. It is suddenly there and you know it!" – Audrey*

Emmanuel's entire journey with God began with journaling.

"I was saved when I was five years old, but I didn't allow God to become Lord of my life until I was seventeen. In my preteen years, I was desirous of God but wasn't willing to let go of the world.

"I was fifteen when I started my prayer writing with God. I don't know why or how it started. The idea just seemed to pop into my head one day. I use a letter "G" in front of what I believe God is saying and a letter "M" in front of my thoughts towards Him. From the beginning, journaling has been a dialogue—a two-way conversation.

"I have been writing down the things God has been saying to me for the past six years. I also write dreams, visions, or pictures I believe God is giving me, as well as the things I'm feeling or sensing. It's neat looking back and examining the

135

things I did right and the things I did wrong. I can also see what hasn't happened yet.

"Before I turned to homosexuality, I wrote in my journal, 'The enemy is knocking at your door.' God was speaking warning after warning to me. I was learning to hear God's voice.

"Journaling was the starting point in my relationship with God. I still have all my prayer journals. If I would lose my Bible, it would be okay because a Bible can be replaced. If I lost my journals, I would feel crushed.

"The psalmists in the Bible gave me the freedom to allow my emotions to come out through journaling. I'm able to process my feelings through writing, being real and honest with myself and God as I write. Journal entries include genuine prayers, 'I'm mad at You! I don't understand!' Freedom in prayer stems from being genuine with God.

> "My prayer closet is wherever my journal is—
> in the basement, at work, in my bedroom,
> or out in the back yard."

"Now my journal also includes a lot of Bible verses and what God is speaking to me through those portions."

Shelly finds journaling both beneficial and frustrating.

"My time with God has changed in some ways, becoming more of a time of listening than seeking His direction. Sometimes I will be on the floor worshiping or sitting quietly. Other times I'll ask, 'What do you want to talk about today?'

"I don't always journal, but I have lots of journals I've started.

I have written many of them during a crisis or deep pain. Each journal represents a specific part of my life. I don't want to go back there, not out of avoidance, but those things are in the past.

"I would like to keep a better record of God's faithfulness to me. We forget how many answers to prayer we have received even though God is faithful all the time. Often, when I have a specific need, God gives me a specific word for it. Over and over, I have seen Him do that. He is so good.

"At times, I feel journaling takes up too much of my time so that not enough time is spent with God, talking to Him. Other times, journaling clarifies my conversation with God. Regardless, writing God's words and the answers helps me to remember how faithful He has been."

Karli's journal has a two-fold function.

"I use my journal as a tool to keep track of what God has said. Whether that's through a prophetic word through somebody else or something God has shown me.

"God is always speaking, but we are not always listening. Journaling is a way for my carnal mind to become remotely organized to how God speaks and what He says. His ways are higher than my ways. His thoughts are higher than my thoughts (Is 55:8-9).

> *"There is no way for me to retain what God has said without writing it down."*

"Secondly, I use my journal to record the things I am frustrated about and that are bugging me regarding what God has spoken. When I am between seasons, not yet where He is taking me, I write His words so I can set them aside. Later, if I want, I can go back over what I have written, usually with more clarity."

Keegan shares his experience,

"In my early twenties, there was a gradual progression in my life. I was learning what God had for me, and what God would do to set me free. I struggled with just receiving from Him. I became more receptive and personal in my prayer life, asking God for His forgiveness and redemption to help me do the right things.

"Going into Life Force sped up the process. It was a close season I had with the Lord. I did a lot of prayer journaling and felt a lot of peace in the process as I wrote out what I felt God was saying.

> *"As a result, I became more proactive rather than reactive in my prayers."*

"I also write prophetic letters from God to myself that flow from soaking or waiting in His Presence and asking Him what He wants to say. Then I write what I feel He is speaking to me. I can go deeper with God because I am taking the time to meditate on the Bible and what He is saying to me."

Amanda F. saw how important including writing was in her devotional time with God, but she found she needed more structure to begin.

"For me, journaling was hard, forcing me to process what I sincerely thought and felt. This required the precious resource of time. I didn't know if journaling would be worth giving my time to or not. Previously, I had been inconsistent, perhaps writing in my journal once a year. Eventually, I forced myself to write, no matter what. To keep myself accountable, I made a note in a day planner if I had journaled that day. I chose the early mornings to create this habit and would set a timer on my phone to write for ten minutes.

"I honestly still find it hard to keep from veering off and thinking about something else while reading the Bible. I kept at it though and soon I looked forward to that half-hour of my routine of reading, writing and listening.

"My writing usually comprises what I read from the Bible and what was highlighted to me. I record the Scripture, then write a question to think about or an observation about what I had read. I ask the Lord what He is thinking and I write that down as well. What I think the Lord is saying is the most precious thing to me.

"Another thing I have tried and appreciate is free-flow writing. I ask God, 'What is on Your heart?' Then I write whatever comes to my mind, even if it makes little sense at the moment. Those words have also been significant to my heart."

Meg's journaling experience has dramatically shifted from season to season.

"For me, journaling initially included putting my faith questions and angst about personal struggles on paper. Writing somehow helped me to sort through my thoughts, exposing them with raw honesty and then leaving them with God.

"Later, journaling became mini personal devotionals. From my daily Bible reading, I would record brief portions of Scripture that seemed to stand out to me. They were verses that touched my heart or caused me to ponder. Personal reflections on the verses and a brief prayer concluded the day's writing.

"Just recently, I've been challenged to eliminate my thoughts and use my journal to write Scripture word for word. I have discovered after years of reading the Bible, I was missing so much of what God was saying to me, Spirit to spirit, through the Word. Slowing down and writing Scripture, instead of only reading and meditating on it, has allowed God to speak to me in an entirely different way.

"I find the conviction of Holy Spirit much more intense as I simultaneously see, speak and write the words. Where once I felt a deeper sense of God's Presence during a two-way dialogue penned on paper, now I listen more intently, allowing His Word to go ever deeper into my easily calloused heart and mind.

"I have desired to be sensitive to His promptings for most of my Christian walk. Yet, after decades of being in fellowship with Him, I'm discovering something even more precious in writing His unaltered Word in my journal. Out of that writing flows fresh prayer dialogue.

"God has given me a great capacity for the Bible, reading it through twice each year. The insatiable hunger for His Word has been matched only by the longing to respond to Him in prayer. This new season of journaling Scripture has intensified my passion for both the Bible and prayer."

Amanda [S.] has discovered multiple benefits to writing.

"As I was learning to hear God's voice more clearly, He led me to something that has become important to my heart—that's journaling. **'Deep calls to deep'** on the pages of my journal (Ps 42:7).

"I've been able to rant on the pages, screaming out in anger or frustration and then obtaining God's peaceful response. I'm able to formulate lessons and remind myself of what God has taught me. That kind of clarity wasn't there before I began journaling. God has also used my hand to write the most beautiful and encouraging love letters to myself.

"Journaling has nearly surpassed other forms of prayer and connecting with God. Through writing, intimacy has been birthed between me and my Abba Father. Every time I journal, there is such a precious treasure waiting for me.

"With journaling, I can enter my dark room, my quiet hard place of war, and the simple act of writing brings revelation. Writing opens me up inch by inch, forcing me to listen to my thoughts. Holy Spirit has a special talent for revealing the lies in my beliefs. He spotlights the hurt I'm holding and how I'm now projecting that pain.

> *"Writing softens my heart and opens my mind to see the wisdom from the Father."*

"I sometimes hold back from writing because I may be clinging to sin or grasping tightly to some inner vulnerability or bitterness. God tenderly whispers to come to Him, but still, I wrestle even while sensing His hand heavy on me.

"I go into those times knowing I will have to release things or repent in those pages. Sin can feel so good at the moment. Praise God, He is not one to allow sin to drag us to our death.

"I thank God every day for my pens and my journal. There between the covers of my journal, He speaks tenderly and brings transformation to my life."

Another reason for journaling is to keep an accurate account of the answers God gives to our prayers. This is a strategic part of Merodee's journaling.

"As I exercised my faith by spending disciplined time with God, I would anticipate my time with Him more. Before I started to pray, I wrote the things I wanted to pray about in my journal, often involving our kids.

"I trusted the Lord to lead me to pray in the Spirit for them. Afterward, there would be little nuggets of revelations and prayer that would come to me. I rapidly saw things I longed for in my children come to pass. I knew the answers were tied to prayer even though I did not understand what I was praying for.

> *"God knew to motivate me, I just needed to see the fruit of prayer in my kids."*

"Something changed in that season. God would speak to me and that was thrilling."

BreAnn also keeps a record of answered prayers.

"A prayer journal has been extremely helpful for me. Most of the entries are of me speaking to God. I have also written music and used it for worship. I own a journaling Bible as well, in which I often draw pictures or journal right in the margins of my Bible.

"One thing prayer journaling is great for is recording the

answers to prayer. I will write in the request and then at the end of the week, I record the answers in red. Lots of time everything is written in red. I clearly see how prayer has been answered in one way or another.

"We have received tons of answers to prayer. I know God has a bigger basket of answers than we even fully recognize."

Unmasking the Myth

Some myths people believe around journaling, recording communication with God, and using written prayers include:
- Written prayers aren't effective.
- An authentic prayer must be spontaneous.
- Writing and journaling take precious time away from prayer.

The Bible is filled with written prayers that are just as powerful today as when they were written. From Genesis to Revelation, prayers are recorded for our benefit to re-present over and over to God.

Emmanuel found the written prayers of the psalmists permitted him to be raw and vulnerable with God Himself. Others have used biblical prayers as succinct petitions and declarations.

Taking biblical prayers and repeating them back to God is like reverse lightning. God's Word is alive and powerful, having lightning strength in our mouths (Heb 4:12). When we repeat God's Word back to Him, these prayers become reverse lightning, striking the mark in the spiritual realm, releasing the answers we need.

There is a sense of vulnerability that occurs as we put ink to paper—a permanence to our thoughts, emotions, and words.

"Then the LORD replied: 'Write down the
revelation and make it plain on tablets
so that a herald may run with it.
For the revelation awaits an appointed time;
it speaks of the end and will not prove false.
Though it linger, wait for it;

it will certainly come and will not delay."
Habakkuk 2:2-3

We may not always understand the full purpose or impact of the things we write. Nonetheless, the value of both writing and using written prayers should never be underestimated.

God gave these instructions to Jeremiah,

" 'This is what the LORD, the God of Israel, says,
"Write in a book all the words I have spoken to you.
The days are coming when I will bring my people
Israel and Judah back from captivity and restore
them to the land I gave their ancestors
to possess," says the LORD.' "
Jeremiah 30:2-3

Seventy years later Daniel read the words of prophecy, praying earnestly for their fulfillment. Jeremiah's obedience to write God's words led to Daniel's prayer which brought God's answer.

It is tremendously encouraging, especially in times of struggle, to look back at God's faithfulness through the pages of our journals. How inspiring it will be for others to someday open those journals and see not just the prayers we prayed, but the way God spoke and the answers He liberally gave.

"Lord, I recognize the more involved I am in any
learning process the more I will retain and maintain
the lessons for later. Help me draw courage from the
vulnerable example of biblical writers to record the
prayers and life lessons that You are teaching me. I put
my hand in Your hand as I write. Use writing in a
new way in my communication with You. I invite
You to speak even as I write. May my written
prayers impact the lives of others."

> *"We are often slow learners. We don't realize at the time how profoundly God is moving until we look back."*
> *– Lois*

***

> *"You have to stop and think once in a while, to appreciate what God has done." – June*

***

> *"Since Grade 7, I have written my prayers and talked to God through journaling. I have seen the results." – Emily*

Notes

1. Elisabeth Sifton, *The Serenity Prayer: Faith and Politics in Times of Peace and War* (New York, Norton, 2003), u.n.

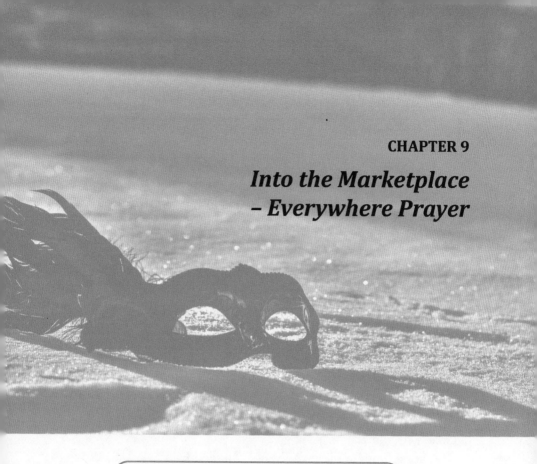

CHAPTER 9

Into the Marketplace
– Everywhere Prayer

*"In you is like a pool or stream. As you pray
in the Spirit, it becomes a fountain
having force, spouting out."*
— Merodee

Although appearances can be deceiving, Nikki didn't fit the stereotype for the charges against her. Slumped in the chair with her head in her hands, her words pulsated between frantic and feeble, "My life is ruined." Not that it was much of a life before. Most of her last few years, she was nearly incapacitated with the painful effects of endometriosis and other ailments.

There was something elusive about her that captured my attention. What was it?

Her whimsical manner?

Her searching eyes?

Her childlike smile?

Her ability to mine joy

from the mountain of despair?

I wasn't sure.

The encounter was brief, yet lingered like dew on my heart. I wondered what labels had crowned Nikki's young life.

Praying during a work shift was not uncommon. Sometimes it took the form of warfare. At other times, I asked God to show Himself merciful and just. Usually, I walked the aisles declaring Bible verses or singing God's love over the incarcerated.

If there was one commonality from shift to shift, cell to cell, prisoner to prisoner, it was the thread of brokenness.

After clocking out, I drove home through the darkness. Usually, a warm shower and the comfort of my bed quickly settles my heart and mind for rest. Tonight, sleep came in fitful spurts. Suddenly, I was jolted awake by a vivid dream, penetrating me with unshakable imagery.

In the dream, I saw what looked like a living room on a penthouse floor of a high-rise building. Open skies created an endless ceiling and transparent walls. Several women, far advanced in years, casually sat in a circle with Nikki.

A song, both audible and visible, descended from high above the blue expanse. In ever-increasing crescendo, it came simple, yet direct in message and melody.

"Behold *her* beauty.

Behold *My* majesty.

Behold *her* beauty,

Behold *My* majesty."

The circle of women applauded both the Singer and the repetitive refrain.

As the song filled the atmosphere, Nikki was transformed before our eyes, becoming younger and more beautiful by the moment. She glowed under the splendor of the Redeemer's voice declaring her worth and His perfection. Ignorant of her miraculous transformation and beauty, she joined the applause of the Creator of His anthem.

On a lower level of an adjacent building, people sat in theatre fashion. Although they saw God's miraculous power indisputably at work, no one here applauded. As if by some invisible electrical current,

148

they were cast face down onto the floor in spasms.

The women who sat around Nikki recognized God's work as the answer to their prayers. With a heavenly mindset, they had interceded for Nikki's true identity to be revealed. Though my few prayers had only recently partnered with theirs, I too could join in the applause over her transformation.

Now fully awake, I felt the weight of conviction for the critical judgments I had formed about Nikki and other prisoners. I knelt on my bed weeping, allowing the whispers of God to penetrate my soul. God showed me how prayer aligns human hearts and people's destinies with holy intention.

All day I prayed with urgency, wanting to tell Nikki about the dream. How would she react? Could I describe the dream in a way she would comprehend?

When I arrived back at work late in the evening, Nikki was resting quietly. Soon she writhed in agony, asking for pain medication.

Sending one last flare prayer Godward, I opened the rectangular bypass slot near the bottom of the cell door and invited, "If you want, Nikki, bring your mat and blanket close. Come. Sit with me. I would like to pray for you."

"Yes, please," she said, as she slid close to the door. Reaching her delicate hand toward mine, she added, "Can you hold my hand? Or . . . no?"

"No," I responded, "but yes, I will." As I held her hand, I prayed the shortest prayer commanding all pain to leave her body and welcoming His peace to come instead. Finally, I told fear to leave. She repeated after me, drawing strength from each word.

Not even a prison door could restrain God from doing what only He can do—connect two women,

> one young, the other old,
> > one bound, the other free
> > > one white, the other dark.

I asked how she was feeling. "I feel calm like I'm being filled with warm water and the pain is completely gone." For a moment, we celebrated by thanking God for His healing power.

"I need to tell you a dream I had about you." Speaking slowly, I allowed my words to penetrate her heart.

149

Her eyes filled with a cautious anticipation as she leaned forward, peering through the tiny opening. I revealed the dream and how God's song transformed her into a young, vibrant, beautiful woman. Her head pressed against the door as between sobs she whispered, "Really? . . . Me? . . . How?"

I told her the old women were intercessors, prayer warriors, who had been praying for her for a long time. She gasped, "When I was three years old, an old grey-haired woman would tell me about Jesus, pray and give me candies."

"All day," she said, "I've been praying God would show me He cares." In those moments, faith wrestled unbelief to silence. The great gulf between God and Nikki dissipated. God was not distant; He was near.

> *"God hears every cry. He hears even the silent cries."* – Jan

Nikki continued, "Three months ago, I had a dream. I had just been released from jail and was going through the streets of the city calling, 'Repent! Jesus is coming! There isn't much time, so get your hearts right with God.' The dream made little sense, but now it makes perfect sense."

We chatted further as trust deepened between us. Nikki talked about one sleepless night a long time ago. She had opened her eyes to see her bedroom fill with Light brighter than any other light. She knew it was Jesus! With mischievous childlikeness, she dramatically pointed her finger and laughed in reminiscence. "Caught You," she had said. "I see You!" Jesus laughed too and before leaving said, "Now go back to sleep."

Confident hope that God would use her to tell others about Him uprooted the last shred of fear. Giving me a contact number and name, she asked, "Please tell my mom about the dream. She will understand."

For a long time, we held hands, crying and laughing together. This one interaction, one moment to share God's love, suddenly made working in the prison a privilege. Working *with* God in my workplace was an honor.

Only God could orchestrate such a prayer initiative.

> One prayer for a stranger
>> led to a dream, which
>>> led to another prayer with a woman
>>>> precious to God's heart.

Only God leads in such unexpected ways, but He needs someone willing to follow.

The next day, I made the call to Nikki's mother, never expecting a response. I was surprised when she called back the following day. "Nikki is at home resting," she said. "She's having some pretty rough moments. If you could come next Monday, Nikki would like to see you."

"Oh! Yes, I'll come!" I could hardly contain my excitement as questions flooded my mind. How could Nikki be home? How could she be free? Monday could hardly come soon enough.

Accompanied by a friend and filled with anticipation, we drove together to see Nikki. The steady swish of the wipers beat a subtle rhythm, backdropping our prayers. Each raindrop signaled a promise God had more to come. Along muddy country roads and across unfamiliar terrain, we traveled to a community a short distance away. As we approached her home, excitement could not and would not be contained.

Without metal bars to restrain us, for the first time we joyfully embraced each other. Neither of us could fully comprehend all God had done in these few days. His supernatural intervention was evident.

Through happy tears, she exclaimed, "I walked around the lake this week. I haven't been able to do that for five years. Look," she said while performing a perfect squat, "I can't do this! I *can't* do this!" Standing erect, she explained, "I had five surgeries on this knee and one surgery on the other. I *can't* do this!" Then beaming from ear to ear, she added, "The endometriosis is completely gone! The pain is all gone."

Each day she was experiencing more of God's healing power. Strength was returning to her body in increments. Nikki had been almost bedridden, "without a life" she had told me, but today hope and purpose-filled her.

"Do you remember the night in jail?" I asked. "You thought your life was ruined."

She nodded silently.

"What you thought was your final moment, the end of everything precious, God designed as a defining moment. In fact, He has turned what you considered your darkest moment into the finest moment in your life. What you believed marked the end, was, in fact, God's beginning of new life with you."

Only God is so loving and gracious, creating divine appointments and redirections. Is this prayer when there is neither beginning nor end? Is this prayer when words and actions melt together, uniting hearts and lives?

> *"At first, I tried to figure prayer out. How? Now I know*
> *I don't need to figure out how. I have no idea how!*
> *God is so big! He has it figured out."*
> *— Charlene*

The gospel accounts of Matthew, Mark, Luke, and John are peppered with workplace encounters with Jesus—fishermen, farmers, doctors, politicians, tax collectors, housewives, military leaders and more. We were never intended to restrict relationship with God to secluded basement rooms, behind stained glass windows, or in members-only Christian clubs.

God is yearning,

    inviting,

        welcoming,

            hoping, and

                expecting

we will take Him along with us wherever we go. Since we spend an enormous part of our time in the workplace, it only makes sense that we welcome Him there too.

Yet, prayer is perhaps most intimidating in our workplace. We may face ostracization, reprimand, or even dismissal for boldly living for Christ. Nonetheless, those who have bravely stepped out in faith have experienced supernatural encounters in the marketplace. They have witnessed God intervene in the lives of others.

Personal Perspectives

As a private business owner, Kevin says making prayer a normal part of doing business has reaped so much fruit.

"I went through my first fifteen years in business, not mingling prayer and work. It was a terrible mistake. I would pray for our productivity and provision, but I was missing the most valuable piece.

"About ten years ago, I realized I had this internal list of people in front of me every day—people I could intercede for. For a long time, people would come into my office because they were maxed out on credit cards, stressed and unable to make payments, or going through marital breakup and watching their businesses in turmoil because of it. I wouldn't even offer to pray for them.

> *"I realized I had this incredible opportunity to be praying for the needs of these people and letting them know I was praying for them."*

"I don't know what the catalyst was to change, but praying for clients has been remarkable. If they're okay with it, I'll even share some prophetic words with them.

"One incident a couple of years ago stands out. A client who previously had suffered from anxiety and depression was applying for life insurance. He wasn't sure if he could get coverage, but the policy we were working on was quite important. I told him I was praying it would get approved faster than anything we had ever applied for. Even though it was in depth in underwriting, it was approved in a week.

153

Within ten days, we had the policy in our hands. I was kind of smug and said, 'I've never seen this happen so fast.'

"I probably tried to overemphasize the power of God in the situation, but he was indifferent. I thought, 'How can that not impact you?'

"About three days later, he phoned, 'I don't know what's going on. I just talked to the doctor; I have prostate cancer.' This policy had gone through only days before the diagnosis. Then I had another opportunity to pray for him for cancer. He has been under medical care and it is in total remission.

"For half my business career, I missed out on those opportunities because I never thought of praying for my clients.

"Now prayer is a regular part of our business. My wife and I call it our business planning with the Lord. We start Monday mornings with an hour or two of prayer. It's our 'First Things First.' We not only line up our week ahead, but we pray and prophesy over each other. We make declarations over our business and our clients.

"I wish I would have prayed like that twenty-five years ago instead of just ten. The fruit of prayer is phenomenal. I didn't know God was interested in every aspect of my life."

Faith and a strong call from God led Clay to prayer ministry, yet he confesses,

"Where I struggle with faith is in finances. I know God met my need yesterday. He promises to meet my needs tomorrow. 'But today, Lord, I'm struggling.'

"I was in the office making up an order, 'How much should we get? How much can we afford? How much do we need?'

154

"A staff member asked, 'Did you pray about it?'

" 'No,' I responded, 'I've never prayed about orders.'

"Well, that day we started praying through orders. For one particular book, we felt we were to order a weird amount. 'Okay Lord, we will order thirty-three.' Those books sat on the shelf for six months. Then a church called to order exactly thirty-three books.

"When we listen to God, it makes sense later. At the moment, however, it might feel a little weird. We learned to be obedient to God in business."

Charlotte, now retired, wasn't shy about disclosing her professional goal. As a teacher, she ultimately wanted to share God's love with her students.

"God taught me to love people. For thirty-three plus years, I loved each one of my students in a very special way. Every morning before schoolwork began, we would open with the Lord's prayer. I taught them to not just recite the prayer, but how to pray. For some children, this was perhaps the only prayer they learned.

"It wasn't in the curriculum, but I felt it was my duty. I believed God put these children in my classroom so I could teach them His principles to live their lives by. Fifty years earlier, prayer and Bible reading would have been very much a part of school life.

> *"There were a lot of circumstances prayed through."*

"The Gideons always came during the Grade 5 year to present New Testaments to the children. We would spend a lot of time going through the books of the Bible. We also allowed them to accept Jesus as their Savior and to enter their name and the date in the back of their Bibles. I didn't care what the school board said.

"I have absolutely no regrets. For some of those children, it may have been their only opportunity to receive Christ and to learn about Him. Some of those children met an untimely death; my prayer is that those in-class moments affected their eternity. I know I will meet a lot of them in Heaven and look forward to that day.

"God's principles never go out of style and are still what He wants us to live by."

Karli also desires to re-present the Gospel of Jesus Christ in every aspect of her life, including her work in the school system.

"I allow the Lord to fill me up in the morning when I'm in that intimate spot with God. I want to walk into school working fully for Him. In my workplace it will be through kind gestures, loving words and sweet actions. As a teacher, I pray over the classroom, for kids who are struggling and for staff members who are hurting or carrying burdens.

"I often play Christian instrumental worship music when my students are working. It allows God to do what He wants without me dishonoring authority.

"I teach math, science, and social studies, but the approach I take is Christ-centered. I want to make sure the kids understand, so I ask God, 'What do I use to teach the multiplication tables? What is the best way to meet their needs academically?'

> *"I combine teaching with prayer,*
> *prophetic acts, and life-giving love.*
> *I could never turn Jesus off and go to work."*

"What I do may seem outrageous, but the kids get it. For example, when teaching about gravity, I asked, 'Lord, what do I use to get them excited about learning that things fall?' He told me to stand on the chair and jump off saying the word 'gravity.' Through spontaneous movement, I felt a shift in the atmosphere. Even if I look foolish, it brings life to our class.

"As a teacher, I see prayer in the classroom as an enormous responsibility. I'm growing and discerning the big pieces God wants me to take home to pray more about. The little prayers I discreetly declare and decree over the kids in the classroom. Whether my prayer is fifteen minutes at home with a lot of detail or less than a minute in the classroom, God will use it either way.

> *"I am called to love and cover every student*
> *and their families in prayer, so God can*
> *do what He wants in each of them."*

"When I see a child looking depressed, I pray quietly, 'Lord, I declare Your life and joy over that child. Depression, you will not have your way, in Jesus' Name.' I've seen children move from sad to joyful through these silent prayers. If we declare things out in faith, God will bring it to pass.

"We get to be the hands and feet of Jesus in our workplace. Doing our jobs through honor and humility becomes a testimony of who Christ is. There is significance in *being* the Gospel—a person of light in the darkness. My job is to lean into Jesus, listening and being obedient. God can use my life and walk to open opportunities, but I don't need to try to make

157

them happen.

> *"If we ask, God will open doors to share Jesus."*

"I used to put a lot of pressure on myself to share the Gospel, knowing everybody needs Jesus. Salvation doesn't come from me; salvation comes from God."

Patrick worked for many years in the mine. It was a tough environment to thrive as a Christian. Two incidents, in particular, proved the difference prayer makes.

"I was praying over my workplace. I felt one way when I left home, then at work, I would feel something different. I was tuned into the reality it wasn't just me.

"One of my operators had an angry outburst that went on and on. I left the room and went up to the highest point of the process plant. I prayed over the atmosphere, asking "God's angels to come and commanded the tormentors to leave. When I came back to where he was, I asked how he was doing. 'Fine!' he said, 'About an hour ago, I started feeling fine.' This guy wasn't a believer in God. When you know what you are praying for, you will see results.

"On another occasion, the process plant I worked in was about to shut down. There were about five different proverbial train wrecks ready to happen all at once. The plant could go down by any of these problems in only five minutes. Other operators and I were all over the plant working to get things straightened out. I prayed, asking God to send angels and straighten things out.

"He knew what was going on and how to change it. Almost immediately things turned around. We were short-staffed. It took a lot of work by everyone doing things throughout the plant, but everything turned around. I know God answered prayer. I had worked at the mine for twenty-six years and had been a supervisor for about five, but that was the worst shape the plant was ever in and yet it pulled out of it. It was an amazing turnaround.

> *"God showing up at work! That's a hoot!"*

"I also prayed for the guys almost every day—sometimes one person specifically or at other times the whole bunch."

God is looking for anyone who will partner with Him.

**"I looked for someone among them
who would build up the wall and stand before me
in the gap on behalf of the land . . ."
Ezekiel 22:30**

Far too often God searches in vain. Isaiah said, **"(God) was appalled that there was no one to intervene"** (Is 59:16).

More and more, ordinary men and women are stepping forward in faith and positioning themselves in the gap for God. Audrey, a beauty consultant, has built her business around prayer.

"One of the main reasons I appreciate the company I've worked for the past twenty-four years is because prayer is engrained in the company. Prayer precedes business gatherings and the last thing on the agenda is thanking God for what He is doing. I have witnessed many leaders pray during seminars, even with thousands of Christians and non-Christians present.

"One special moment happened a few years ago. I had tried several times to meet with a specific lady. Each time, she canceled our appointment because her daughters could not be there. Finally, when she phoned to cancel once again, I said, 'Why don't I come over anyway just to meet you?'

"She was a quiet lady, so I was trying to start a conversation. I asked her about her Easter plans. She said, 'My kids are coming, and it's my granddaughter's third birthday.'

"When I said, 'That's exciting,' she quickly turned her head away. I knew she was crying.

" 'She has brain cancer. The doctors said she would never make her third birthday.'

"I stopped everything; we prayed together. Not just a minute prayer—we prayed! Afterward, we stood at the door and prayed again.

"As much as I tried, I couldn't connect with her again. Through the intervening years, the enemy wanted to tell me the little girl died. Each time I thought of her I would pray again, 'No, God! You take care of her.'

"Several years passed, but about a year ago at a ladies' event, a woman approached me and introduced herself. She looked familiar, but I couldn't remember her name. She said, 'I just wanted to say my granddaughter is alive and well today.'

"When your antenna is up, God opens prayer opportunities."

"I've prayed with many others through work regarding their marriages and children. I don't know if I could work in a business where I couldn't pray with people. If I had to only do what I do for business, I would have been out of it a long time ago."

160

As a young man, Dennis prayed for God's direction whether to enter medicine or the pastorate. God called him to both. Dennis and his wife, Betty, are a powerful prayer team. He shared about a couple of God-given opportunities he has experienced as a physician.

"The first day back doing a locum tenens medicine in Inuvik, Northwest Territories, a lady I knew from the church came to see me. She had lost about forty pounds and looked frail. The change in her quite surprised me. I knew she had multiple serious chronic medical conditions, and she was on multiple medications. Yet at the end of the consultation, I had no clue what was going on. I ordered lab tests, but the cause of her illness wasn't clear. I don't specifically recall praying.

"In the middle of the night, I woke up with a diagnosis in my mind. I had only seen one patient with that disease I had personally diagnosed previously, and she didn't even fit the description completely. She had fainted twice in the last week; I was aware if this was her condition, any kind of trauma could cause death. I was so disturbed, I went to the hospital and tried to phone her.

"In the morning, I was able to contact her. I told her, 'We have to start you on treatment as if this is the diagnosis until we know for sure.' She immediately responded to the treatment.

"I ordered other blood tests done. It would take ten days to two weeks to get the report back. Two tests had to be sent away, since we couldn't do them in Inuvik. Ultimately, we received the report confirming her diagnosis.

"Betty knew when I got up at one o'clock in the morning, (and not being on call) it was a matter of life and death. It was God who showed me the diagnosis.

"After her diagnosis was verified, and she saw a specialist who confirmed and began the ongoing management of her illness, she told me her mom had said, 'Go to Dr. Boettger. Betty prays for him and you will get an answer.' She also told me the specialist had said, 'You shouldn't be alive.'

"I said to the woman, 'This is a sign of how much God loves you. He loves you so much He would connect all this and get a diagnosis for you.'

"There was another revelatory event. They called me to the hospital to see someone with persistent vomiting. I picked up my stethoscope and walked to emergency to see him.

> *"The Lord said, 'Faith is like a stethoscope. You have to plug your ears to everything else to hear the heart of God.' "*

"I was marveling at that when I went to see my patient. As I was interviewing him, the Lord dropped the diagnosis into my mind. People who have that problem end up with episodes of continuous vomiting. CT (computed tomography) scans and other tests don't reveal the issue, making the diagnosis difficult. The Lord alone gave me the diagnosis. I looked it up later and he exactly fit the picture of a variant form of migraine. I had never seen a patient with this diagnosis, to my knowledge.

> *"It is something when God will use you as a vessel. The honor and glory are for God."*

" 'When we were in McLennan, where Dennis practiced for twenty-five years,' Betty added, 'I would do book work and then some afternoons go have coffee with the nurses. They would all tell stories of some occasions when Dennis didn't know what the diagnosis was, but he came up with the diagnosis through a word of the Lord. The nurses saw and witnessed this on several occasions.' "

Unmasking the Myth

Today we blast the erroneous myth that prayer is unwelcome in the workplace. Quite the opposite is true, although sensitivity to others and the workplace environment is important.

Many people of multiple ethnicities view prayer as a sincere extension of care and concern. People don't need to share our Christian faith or belief system to experience God's love. God is much bigger than that!

A woman in the Bible approached a well in the heat of the day to draw water. She chose a time when no one else would be present to gaze, ridicule or criticize her. At first glance she doesn't appear courageous, but brave she was.

Here, in the middle of her mundane work activity, she encountered Jesus. He chose her to be the first person to reveal Himself as the Messiah. She left her water pot and ran into town telling everyone about Him. Throughout the marketplace, the coffee shops, private homes and calling down the open streets she went. **"Because of the woman's testimony"** almost the entire town showed up to see Jesus for themselves (Jn 4:39).

Jesus used the marketplace to
call people into full-time ministry,
heal the sick and deliver the bound,
teach those who would listen,
welcome the lost, and
befriend the outcast.

The religious leaders tried to make the house of God a marketplace. The fear of becoming unclean kept them from taking God *to* the people. Jesus took the Presence and power of God to everyone and anyone, wherever He found them.

Work, in its different forms, is mentioned approximately eight hundred times in the Bible. That's more than all the words used to express worship, music, praise, and singing combined. God cares about where we work and the people we work with and for.

Incorporating prayer into the workplace begins before we leave for work. Our daily devotions of reading the Bible and praying over our workplace establishes the right tone in our hearts. Then like Dennis, in the right moment, God will give us the answers to serious problems because we remain sensitive to His voice.

Marketplace experiences are diverse. Like Patrick, we might need to find a quiet spot to pray, asking God's help for a situation. We can all be alert to raise our spiritual antennas like Audrey, prepared to pray for those in need.

Let's ask God to help us see opportunities for prayer where we work. He may even prompt us to make a radical shift in the way we do business. Like Kevin, we may want to incorporate prayer as a "First Things First" business strategy.

> **"Finally, be strong in the Lord and in
> His mighty power."**
> **Ephesians 6:10**

"Lord Jesus, I thank You for the privilege of working with others. Prepare my heart early in the morning to be alert to opportunities to pray for others. Increase my faith to trust You more. May I be increasingly aware of how much You love the people I encounter in the workplace. May I love others with the same love, desiring for them to meet You and discover Your love for themselves."

"Believe more! Trust more!" — Charlene

***

"God can use anyone who is willing." — Betty

***

> "Prayer is a partnership. God has asked me to partner with Him—releasing the His will, Kingdom, and domain on the earth."
> – Emmanuel

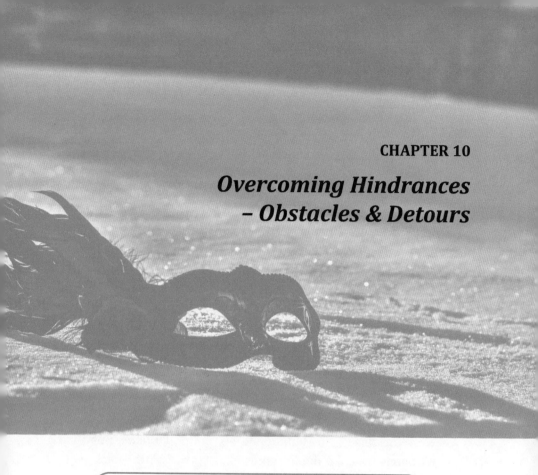

CHAPTER 10

Overcoming Hindrances
– Obstacles & Detours

> *"If God asks for something to be sacrificed, whether*
> *it is bad or good, it is always because He*
> *has the best ahead for us."*
> *— Amanda* [S.]

Ryker bounced from his room with the usual light spring to his step and a mischievous grin spread from ear to ear. "Is this the day I get my pony?" he asked as he slid up to the table for breakfast.

His parents' shocked glances at each other conveyed the same question, "Where did he get that idea?" Since Ryker had never mentioned a pony before, they assumed he must have been dreaming about horses in the night.

After school, with the same joyful anticipation, Ryker's words entered the house even before he did, "Is it here? Was today the day my pony came?"

The next morning was a repeat; the afternoon a perfect copy. Every day he awoke with expectation, believing today was *the* day. Days turned into weeks; weeks turned into months. Still, he didn't waver. Never was he discouraged by a negative response.

Over a year later, Ryker arrived home from school with his usual query, "Was today the day? Did my pony come today?"

Dad ruffled Ryker's already mussed hair, "Go change your clothes; I need your help with the chores."

Ryker hummed a tune as he disappeared into his bedroom. It wasn't long before he reappeared, "I know my pony will soon be here," he announced.

"Come with me, son," his dad said. "Today's the day!"

His father's words trailed somewhere behind Ryker who was already out the door and climbing into the truck. Dad followed trying hard to contain his enthusiasm as Ryker chatted non-stop. The father-son team headed into town together to pick up a few supplies, thoroughly enjoying each other's company.

Arriving back home, they stopped in front of the barn to unload the truck. Ryker hurried ahead to open the barn door. "What? I knew it!" he shouted as he jumped up and down like a pogo stick. His feet barely touched the ground as he scurried to the back stall. "I knew it! I just knew it!"

Ryker and Dusty warmed to each other instantly, proving to be a suitable match. There may never have been a pony so loved.

I'm not sure I have heard of another story of such compelling faith and unquestioning trust as Ryker's. He knew where to make his request. He also knew someday, somehow, his request would be answered. Ryker kept asking, not presumptuously, but with joy, knowing his dad intended to provide.

It was up to Ryker's father to respond. Ryker's faith never wavered; his enthusiasm never waned. He was as sure on day four hundred as he was on day four his father had heard his request. He knew his father was generous, loving, and trustworthy with the timing and outcome.

But what happens when the pony doesn't arrive? What do we do when God's answer is "No!" or "Wait!"

When sickness strikes or

the divorce is final?
When bankruptcy knocks or
death robs?
When tears fill the night and
joy becomes a faint memory?
What do we do with unanswered prayer, lingering pain, or mounting disappointment? What do we do with prayer then?

> *"Every problem can be solved through prayer."*
> *— Caleb*

Even though we know His thoughts and His ways are much higher than ours, life is difficult and disappointments are hard to accept. We cannot diminish the struggle while overcoming obstacles and navigating detours. The potential of shipwrecking our faith, ditching our devotion, or pausing our prayers looms during these times.

Personal Perspectives

Candice shared a little about keeping a pure heart.

"Outside of my family, I never felt connected with others. My heart always wanted deeper friendships with people than what I was experiencing. I felt weary of the spiritual atmosphere even in a Christian school. I kept trying, but was feeling burnt out and lonely without a relational community with people who loved Holy Spirit.

"My prayer language began in tongues when I was three years old, but praying in English was always a block for me. From eighteen years old on, I didn't want to pray and felt handicapped in prayer. I didn't know how to articulate the right words to pray.

"A couple of years later, a pastor told me, 'When you are praying in tongues, you are praying the mysteries the Spirit is speaking in your heart.' He also advised me to pray Paul's prayers for the churches.

"I began to journal and sensed more what the Spirit was saying. English often came as a translation to tongues. I would hear a word or see a picture and then speak it out in English. It wasn't automatic.

> *"God took me on a journey in prayer, recognizing my weaknesses and giving me keys past my handicaps."*

"The first time someone asked me to lead in corporate prayer, I went into a corner. God said, 'Instead of looking at yourself and trying to find words to say, look at Me and My throne declaring the truth about who I am.' God gave me the key to overcome!

"Lack of intimacy with the Lord in my prayer time usually shows a resistance because of pride. The Bible says God resists the proud (Jm 4:6 NKJV). When we come to Him with a contrite heart, recognizing our need for Him, He comes quickly to us. When we don't sense God's Presence, He might be waiting, allowing us discomfort while He is getting our hearts right.

"We need to let God bring hope. God is good and turns even grave situations around for our good. It isn't enough to know it in our heads, but it's important to keep discouragement and disappointment out so we can believe it in our hearts.

"When we've been through awful experiences, it's hard to believe God is good. As we choose to let go of disappointment and trust God, it engages our faith. Even when I don't have the answers yet, I'm not going to compare this time in my life to what was or what will be."

Isaac's obstacles to prayer were independence and shyness.

"I have to remind myself to trust in God rather than in myself. In university when I needed God's help, I said, "After I get this done, then I will have a relationship with You."

"Too often, I pray about something and then try to do it myself. When that happens, I'm exalting myself above the work of God, but God doesn't want us to forget Him in the process.

"God only shows me enough for the next step. He doesn't want me focused on where I'm going, but to continue praying, waiting on Him and watching how He unfolds things in my life. Prayer has to be a lifestyle, giving everything to the Lord, trusting Him to take care of it. Praying for everything is humbling, nerve-wracking, and challenging. Sometimes there's nothing to be said!

> *"Just being in God's Presence is enough.*
> *I want it to be enough all the time."*

"When praying over people, I have to get over my shyness and fear of what others think. It helps to know God wants to see people saved and healed even more than I do. I know Jesus loves everyone He leads me to pray for. His love is amazing!

"He gives me the faith and boldness I need. The Bible tells us to make sure our faith is in God alone. Just saying, 'In Jesus' name' isn't enough, but I have to examine my heart to be sure my faith is in Him. I take time and wait on the Lord to allow me to see if it isn't.

"God will help us overcome any obstacle. For me, humility, which comes from knowing how great God is, is the key.

Prayer isn't about us!"

One of the biggest obstacles Kate faced was the busyness of life.

"Hindrances to prayer can come in many ways. Sometimes it comes even through believers who don't understand the urgency of prayer.

"We constantly have to overcome thoughts that try to convince us to get other things done instead of responding to the urging of Holy Spirit. Daily routine and the busyness of life can easily intrude on our prayer time.

"The first thing I do when I realize there is a hindrance is to cry out, 'Help Lord! How do I deal with this?'

"Once we understand the importance of prayer, we know it is a priority over everything else. It's a matter of obedience in deciding to follow the lead of Holy Spirit. When we discipline ourselves to spend a certain part of our day in prayer, waiting on the Lord, fasting or whatever, God provides a way for us to spend time with Him.

"As a young mom with small children, finding time with the Lord was difficult. I cried out, 'Lord, give me even five minutes with You without interruption.' When I asked the Lord for help, I saw periods of time when I could get alone with Him. Holy Spirit guided me, showing me how to have those daily times of prayer."

Patrick overcame both home and work situations to pursue a prayer lifestyle.

"Because of life circumstances, I drifted away from God and didn't pray for quite a few years. I was going through a tough time in my marriage. I didn't think God was interested; I didn't give Him the credit of being able to restore my marriage. I became hard-hearted and stopped praying. After my divorce, I came back full circle, giving my life to the Lord and being baptized. I knew it wasn't just a Sunday thing; I gave myself to Him, period. That drastically changed my prayer life.

"It can be extremely isolating when you work among unbelievers and are trying to be the only spark of fire there. It's a dry place when no one understands how you feel and how compelled you are toward the Lord. It's easy to become too busy and justify why you didn't pray or seek the Lord that day.

"Either unbelief or not knowing what is on God's menu for us can also keep us from praying. For me not knowing what is available through prayer can be a big hindrance to consistently praying. We can each go around the prayer circle not fully knowing what is available to us.

"If we don't know we are sons and daughters of a good Heavenly Father, it hinders our prayers. Not knowing God's will can be another obstacle we face. We may be praying our own will either unknowingly or sometimes selfishly. These can easily hinder our prayer walk, in one way or another."

For Amanda ^{C.} a call to foreign missions interrupted her prayer routine.

"Everything I had previously relied on to keep me full of God suddenly was shut down. It left me with just God, but I wasn't hearing Him in a way I had before. I questioned what was going on.

"I expected to take the Presence of God wherever I went, but everything was different in this unfamiliar country. I wasn't able to get alone with God to read my Bible or worship. I felt abandoned, like God walked away and left me.

"God showed me I had been substituting worship for His Presence. I needed my foundation back on the Word of God. I came across the verse, **'Never will I leave you; never will I forsake you,'** and **'I will not leave you as orphans'** (Heb 13:5, Jn 14:18).

"Even though I wasn't feeling God's closeness, I chose to believe God's Word and told my heart it was true. Eventually, my heart followed His truth.

"I hadn't slept well in weeks and my health was suffering. I could handle the sleeplessness and sickness, but I couldn't handle not sensing the Presence of God. I needed God to bring that back.

> *"Not being able to hear God is probably the biggest struggle."*

"When I talk with someone and they don't answer, I wonder what's the point. Without intimacy with God, it was a dark time of my soul. I view intimacy and hearing God as interchangeable. I missed having the ability to spend time with God one-on-one. Jesus said, 'How do you think I felt when I left Heaven and was born here? I left the glory.'

"My journey back to prayer and intimacy began by forcing myself to read the Bible again."

Christie mentioned other hindrances to prayer.

"The simplest thing that hinders prayer is lethargy or mental fatigue. I often want to get up in the middle of the night to pray, but can't get past the hurdle to do it.

"Other times, I'm self-conscious, worrying about the right words to pray and end up mumbling. I have to get past thinking about myself or what other people think. When prayer feels awkward and uncomfortable, I can wonder, 'What's the point?'

"If I'm not ready for God's answer, I'll decide not to pray at all. Honestly, there are some things I deliberately hesitate to pray about, because I know when I hear God, I must act on it. Once I start the process in prayer, it's going to be work.

"At other times the topic feels huge. It isn't something I can brush under the mat or pray about for a few minutes in the car. When I feel like I need to give prayer a good chunk of time, it is easy to forget about it or busy myself with other things.

"Sometimes, we can think one prayer is enough, question why we are even praying, or say, 'God knows my heart; I don't need to pray.' We forget that for certain things we need to persist."

> *"Over and over in our prayer journey, we have the answers and the seemingly unanswered." – Merodee*

Kristina and Kimberly shared how feeling inadequate in prayer can be a hindrance.

Kristina began,

"Perhaps one ongoing struggle in prayer is to overcome inadequacies. First thinking, 'Who am I?'—then swinging to the other end of the spectrum with pride and God bringing me through a bit of humbling.

175

> *"When we get a glimpse that prayer isn't about us, but yet God sees us a lot bigger in Him than we see ourselves, prayer changes."*

"It's pretty cool when we realize our significance in Him and the Kingdom. If we shrink back from prayer out of inadequacy, we are not as effective as we could be."

Kimberly said,

"That's an area where Kristina and I encourage each other often. One thing that frustrates me is when I will step out in an honest place of confidence and authority in prayer, then I experience pushback. It is usually a pushback against my identity. For me, it's an ongoing struggle. Yet, God continues to show me the impact of my prayers. They really are powerful and effective."

Kristina added,

"Sometimes we overcome through obedience. When we feel the Lord nudging us to step out and pray for this person or do that thing, just doing it is sometimes enough to break that feeling of inadequacy."

Kimberly agreed,

"Another way of exposing the inadequacy is speaking encouragement. I value when I can honestly share where I am feeling inadequate and have someone alongside me speaking honest encouragement."

Kristina half-jokingly laughed,

"Stomping around sometimes helps."

Kimberly said,

"I often sleep on it. Sometimes I can have this discouraging day, go to bed and God seems to break through. The next day I wake up with more vigor, faith, and the answers I was needing! Often, the more I try to figure things out, the more I cycle downward. Don't try to figure it out; pray and then sleep on it."

Kristina shared one more point,

"Worship works too. Worship gets our eyes off of ourselves and back onto God who is powerful. Prayer is about Him. Worship often propels us to where we need to go in prayer."

Emily shared briefly,

"God continues to give me more understanding of prayer and warfare. For about three months, I felt like my prayers were blocked because of unforgiveness. I kept praying, but I knew I wasn't breaking through. I didn't even know I was carrying hurt. Once I forgave, the blockage to prayer broke, and things improved.

"Another hindrance to prayer arises when our bodies are physically tired; then the mind becomes a spiritual battleground. The mind and spirit are connected. God wants to build our spiritual muscles of both mind and spirit."

Keegan shared other problems he's encountered.

"Until young adulthood, most of my prayers were repenting and begging God to not smite me. I felt I had to perform or measure up. I didn't have spiritual freedom and was doing

177

things I didn't want to do and not doing what I wanted to do.

"Though I was involved in church, I felt separated and was suffering from depression, shame, and distress. As hard as I tried, I could not get away from judgment and comparing myself to others.

> *"Comparison will always bring us down,*
> *killing creativity and joy."*

"One time there were circumstances out of my control. I was feeling hurt by friends and started yelling at God, being raw and real. Afterward, I heard God speak to me in a soft, gentle voice. Even in my lack of humility and reverence, He met me where I was, showing me gentleness and understanding. When we truly seek God looking for answers, He will respond.

"Because of insecurity, I experienced a dark period when I stepped into temptation and sin. Filled with shame, I felt I had gone too far and couldn't approach perfect God anymore. Pride and insecurity kill prayer. They are *me* focused instead of God-focused. In prayer, we see how great God is not how great we are."

If you are feeling disappointment with God or unanswered prayer, take time alone and be honest with Him about what you are struggling to understand and believe. To keep a clean slate with God, quickly confess and repent of any accusations you may feel toward Him. We are invited to draw to His throne of grace with confidence (Heb 4:16).

Here is a simple prayer to pray:

> *"Father, I know You are always good and will never*
> *abandon me. I am feeling discouraged and disappointed.*
> *It feels like I'm alone and forgotten. It doesn't feel like*

You are keeping Your promises to me. I need Your help.
Heal my broken heart and deliver me from this place
of discouragement. Thank You, Lord."

> "God doesn't waste anything, not even the mistakes.
> He uses it all." – Shelly

Dawn shared,

"Often when I was distant from God, I still wanted to spend time with Him. Other times, I forgot about Him altogether, letting life crowd Him out.

"Alcohol was God's competition in my life. Sometimes it pushed me toward Him; other times I would get a buzz on to avoid feeling. My addiction numbed me from anxiety and fear. By my thirties, I firmly had set the habit of drinking regularly and shoving all those feelings aside.

"I went for a long time without communicating with Him. I thought, 'God, You know what will happen anyway. I will catch up to You on the other side.' It was fatalistic!

"Relationship with God is about laying it all down, surrendering, and asking God for help. I finally gave God my all.

"However, one of my problems today is when I try to be still and pray, my mind drifts all over the place. I struggle to focus and start daydreaming; my eyes are open but my brain turns off. If my heart isn't connected to God's heart, my prayer life is very dry and I end up just asking for things. Then it isn't about my relationship with God or love for those around me."

Everyone faces challenges when pursuing a vibrant prayer walk. As well as those already shared, other people mentioned:

- Doubting the ability to hear God or be connected with Him
- Feeling guilty about not praying the right way or long enough
- Unforgiveness and unhealed wounds
- Affluence and lack of genuine need

The enemy will use a wide variety of things to keep us from the place of prayer.

Joy-Lyn has developed a novel approach to difficulties.

"I consistently challenge myself, knowing I *don't* need to be more talented, but I *do* need to grow in character. In Romans, Paul tells us trials produce perseverance, which produces character and ultimately gives us hope (Rom 5:3-4).

"I pray, 'Lord, if trials are how I gain character, I want more trials in my life. I want to embrace trials, so give me challenges.' God answers those prayers quicker than any other.

> *"It would be wrong to say God will never bring correction or be sharp with us. He always encourages and builds us up, but it usually goes hand in hand with a challenge."*

"I will not say God puts difficulties in my life, but I wonder how much the Lord protects us because we resist trials rather than embracing them. How many more trials could we endure and grow in? Yet, at the same time during the trial, I cry, 'O Lord, this is so hard.'

"The first benefit I've experienced through trials is my dependency on the Lord has increased. Second, emotional stability and maturity have been a by-product of the challenges I've faced. Through the trials, the Lord has encouraged me to not live by my emotions or let the enemy bring chaos. I'm learning to not let anything rob me of joy.

"We all need to learn how to persevere through trials and suffer well. Trials are normal. It isn't a matter of *if* I suffer, but do I suffer *well?*"

Unmasking the Myth

I've hit a few obstacles of my own. Sometimes even a pea-sized quandary triggers a gigantic reaction. Other times a mountain-sized impasse barely registers on my impact scale. Why?

It rests in my perception of being able to overcome. If there is any hesitation, the enemy shouts, "You are NOT ENOUGH for THIS!" Too often whether knowingly or unknowingly, I chorus his assessment.

I'm not good enough,
    strong enough,
        pure enough,
            loved enough,
                whole enough,
                    full enough,
                        wise enough,
                            free enough
to prevail against my circumstances. I'm not near enough to God to pray or expect an answer.

Ryker knew the goodness and kindness of his father. He trusted in his father's loving nature and ability to provide. When we believe in our hearts how great the goodness and kindness of our Heavenly Father is, we quickly stomp that ugly myth into the dust. We will never be enough, but God is. He will always be
    good enough,
        strong enough,
            loving enough,
                whole enough,
                    full enough,
                      wise enough,
                        free enough to

fill us with confidence and our prayers with supernatural power. With His last breath Jesus said, **"It is finished!"** Whatever we need, God has already provided it for us.

God surrounds our inadequacy with His perfect love and grace.

> **"That is why, for Christ's sake, I delight in weaknesses, in insults, in hardships, in persecutions, in difficulties. For when I am weak, then I am strong."**
> **2 Corinthians 12:10**

Understanding the intimate relationship we have with our Father produces a childlike quality of anticipation and hope, like Ryker, that thrives in all circumstances. Then we can continually draw close as we rest, wait and trust in God alone. We are free to be weak while relying on His strength.

One of my hardest life seasons occurred during a collision of heart-wrenching events: my father had fought a terminal illness for many years and was now palliative; our son broke his neck in an automobile accident; our marriage appeared irreparably broken and needed nothing short of a miracle.

I could choose to either run from faith or sink deeper into it. By God's grace, I chose the latter. This broken place proved to be the refining fire of purification separating the dross from the gold in significant areas of my life.

Eventually, I responded to God's invitation to a fellowship with Him which was purer and sweeter than I had previously imagined. Prayer became a place of joyful waiting in His Presence rather than contending for a breakthrough.

Difficulties, like ominous thunderclouds billowing, swirling and gathering force, roll through our lives in an equally imposing fashion. One never knows the intensity of their onslaught as the eerie dark canopy looms overhead. However, when the storm and danger have passed the rain-soaked air feels fresh. The sun reappears to show the majestic beauty of the retreating clouds.

When we continue in prayer, God will show Himself strong on our behalf. He will see us through to the other side. Whatever hindrances we face, through prayer we will become richer, wiser, and stronger.

Is today the day?
Will Your promise come through today?
Will we trust in the goodness of God?
Today could be the day! With anticipation, pray and believe!

"Thank You, Lord, for the privilege and open door of prayer. Thank You for Your patience and love, drawing me through difficulties, past hindrances and over any obstacles in my way. Your grace and mercy draw me back and back again into Your Presence. You are good, and You do good. With thanks and praise, I come to the place of prayer and intimacy with You."

"We often lower God to meet our pain. If we get anchored in the Word, we can bypass diminishing God in any way."
— Emmanuel

***

"We give the enemy too much power. When something bad happens, we say it was the devil. It may be God putting something into our lives so we will deal with things."
— Kevin $^{W.}$

***

"I don't know what tomorrow holds, but I know who holds tomorrow." — *Charlotte*

CHAPTER 11

Strength in Struggle – The Night Season

> *"To pray without ceasing is a conscious awareness
> of our relationship with God in
> all things at all times."*
> *– Isaac*

Tears fell silently, unabated, an unstoppable stream. The passing of years has neither soothed the pain nor offered answers. The agony of that day burns deep as she forces words through wounded memory, recounting the events.

"It's Dad . . . I think . . . it's . . . a heart attack . . ." her mother's broken words through the phone trailed into silence.

Her first instinct was to form a circle of prayer with her small children. Then, along with her husband, they sped to the family farm. All the way, she pleaded, begged and petitioned God, pushing against the seriousness of her mother's words, "The ambulance is on the way."

They paved every mile along the road home with fervent prayer. Others were quickly called to join the family in faith-filled unison, pressing Heaven's gates for mercy, grace, and healing.

They sped into the yard to her waiting mother, "He's gone." The words crashed against hope like rocks tumbling into a deep abyss. Courage and anger, resolve and disbelief, faith and fear, swirled into inseparable agony.

With unswerving faith, she walked over to the parked ambulance, placing her hands on the closed doors. Once more she stood her ground against death's fierce grip, looking to only God for help. She prayed for breath to miraculously return to her father's lifeless body concealed beyond her reach. Since childhood, she had heard the biblical accounts of others raised from the dead. "Just one more time, God. One more time."

"It's too soon. He's too young. Not now! Why God?" Her raw honesty flailed at the invisible, now silent, God, "Just this one prayer! That's all I ask! Just this one!"

Without answers, numbness temporarily masked the crumbling edifice of once-strong faith. Her father's death reaffirmed her underlying belief God was distant, harsh and perhaps even cruel. Her circumstances only confirmed His cold indifference. Who could trust such a wild, reckless, and uncontrollable God?

Yet somehow, she knew. She knew, though she struggled to believe, God is and always will be loving, gentle, and kind.

> *"If intimacy is not the goal, unanswered prayer cannot be reconciled." — Merodee*

One commonality unites those who courageously share their stories —the thread of suffering. We all live with the uncontrollable presence of suffering and loss. The source of our pain varies, but the list is long, including

depression, suicide and mental illness,

sickness, accident and injury,

trauma, addiction and oppression,

loneliness, rejection and abandonment,

brokenness of body, soul, and spirit.

In the silence of God unanswered prayer remains a mystery lingering unresolved and unexplained.

> *"We have fallen for the lie that says bad things shouldn't happen to good people. The worst thing in the world happened to the best Person in the world when Jesus was crucified. We need to understand it isn't about getting our way or having perfect circumstances, but about continuing to follow Him during our trials."*
> *– Jennifer*

Personal Perspectives

With unparalleled transparency, Lowell and Staci share their prayer journey through struggle. Lowell grew up seeing miracles in a Christian home where faith was strong and prayer fervent.

At age fifteen, Staci wanted to know what it truly meant to be a Christian.

"God just woke me up spiritually. I always had a hunger to know more about God and wasn't always satisfied with the answers I was given."

Lowell said,

> *"God puts us through things to strengthen our faith and relationship with Him. Sometimes that thing is a desert; sometimes it is suffering."*

"I prayed for years, 'God, I want to be closer to You.' He answered that prayer, but not in the way I wanted. I believe God used cancer as a suffering to bring me closer to Him. I tell people, 'Fall on the Rock before the Rock falls on you' (Mt 21:44).

"It took me three rounds of cancer to get where I'm consistent in my devotion time with God. Consistency helps make me become more aware of God's closeness. It also makes it easier to listen to God and tell when it's God speaking. I need time with Him to feel anchored at the beginning of my day."

Staci said,

"Bouts of cancer never created instability in my relationship with God. I ran right to His feet. I was on the floor a lot talking to Him. We had great chats! The first two times Lowell was diagnosed with cancer, my anxiety went through the roof. God didn't take the deep anxiety away. He was building a new foundation about my beliefs in Him and what I thought life should be like.

"Lowell was only thirty-nine years old when he was first diagnosed. The idea of him not being here anymore was not something we expected to confront that early in life. I desperately wanted cancer to go away. When I talked to God, I just wanted Him to say everything would be okay and Lowell would be healthy. God didn't say that to me, but He did say everything would be okay.

"I thought, 'Yeah, but Your version of okay and my version of okay are totally different sometimes. I've read the Bible; I know what Your version of okay looks like.'

"It took a while for God to get me to where I could say,

> " *'You are with me and because You are with me,*
> *it will be okay.'* "

"I think we had to have those experiences so we would have our Ebenezers to look back on (1 Sm 7:12). Since we have been through this, we can say, 'Look how God walked with us through it!' There will always be an element of wrestling. But now, it is much easier to say, 'God! You are enough because You have been enough.'"

Lowell said,

"I know prayer has to be the Holy Spirit's work, but I encourage people to just get together with God even if you don't feel anything. Faith grows faith. The Holy Spirit is a gentle teacher.

"A few years ago, I began to understand and feel the love of God. Even though I had been a Christian my entire life, my relationship with God went up to another level. Going through cancer has amped up knowing and experiencing God to a huge degree.

"There is a marked difference in how strong God is working in my heart. I am glad to have gone through cancer for the growth I've experienced in my relationship with Him. Now I'm continually in conversation with Him throughout the day."

Staci adds,

"God has brought us to understand our walk with Him is all about His goodness and His grace.

> *"The more I learn His heart,*
> *the more I seek His Presence.*
> *The more I seek His Presence,*
> *the more I will know His heart."*

"Everything is about God and His sovereignty so much more than we understand."

Lowell affirms,

"The shift in understanding God's sovereignty—He's in control of more than I ever thought—helped me to rest in Him. I know more now what trust in God is.

"God was preparing us through the testimony of others. When I heard people talk about their relationship with God, their closeness with Him was inspiring. In 2012, when cancer hit, we had nothing else to hang onto but God. We went desperately to Him with an intense closeness."

Staci said,

"The biggest thing I am learning is to be conversational in prayer. Now instead of bringing a list of things I want Him to do, I spend time talking and listening. His responses to me aren't usually gold, glory, and skies filled with singing. It is a normal conversation.

> *"The problem isn't whether God speaks; the problem is will I listen for what He is saying. If I know what He is saying, then I have to be willing to do what He wants me to do."*

Lowell agreed,

"Learning to pause and listen has benefited our whole family. Praying like this was eye-opening for our girls too. They've mentioned how two-way conversations with God helped change their prayer lives.

"The third bout with cancer took me to a level of anxiety I never had before. Anxiety is not something you can just pray away, talk away, or think away. It's there.

"However, I can change how I think with a perspective shift.

Listening to Christ-centered music points me to Jesus and leads me to thank God in prayer. The music lifts my spirit. Taking everything to God right away and being thankful is an awesome thing—a living relationship."

Staci said,

"What do you do when your relationship with God isn't easy? One of the things we've encouraged our girls to do is just keep talking to Him. Keep going to the Word."

Dawn also shared about the struggles along her prayer journey. She possesses a steadiness and maturity beyond her years—qualities gained at a high price.

"I think I've always had a sense of God's Presence. When I was about eight years old, we were living in chaos with my drug-addicted father. I was frustrated in my spirit. People would pick us up and take us to church. I remember praying, 'I want to be a good girl, but maybe I won't try to be good anymore.'

"God heard my cry for help. A little while later, my sister and I were living at my grandparents' house. I remember sitting on the couch being told my father was dead. I heard a scream coming from somewhere, only to realize the surreal sound was coming from deep inside me.

"Filled with confusion and pain, I spent a lot of time hiding in my bedroom alone with my Bible. At church we sang songs based on Bible verses, then at home, I would find and read those verses again. I never thought I heard the Lord speak to me, but I often talked to Him and knew He was real.

"After high school, I felt God's invitation to attend Bible school

191

where I heard God speak at different times. My sister back at home was struggling. God showed me a picture of how rebellion grieves His heart.

"God hurts *with* us, *for* us and *by* us.

"In my twenties, I married an unbelieving spouse. While our two children were still small, I attended university. Life was busy, sometimes crowding God out. Other times, I was focused on Him and needed Him. Quiet times were a peaceful recharge in prayer and reading the Bible as I enjoyed His Presence and felt He was enjoying mine too.

"As deep unhappiness filled my marriage, my heart began shutting down toward my husband who wanted to be both single and married. We were living under the same roof but distant. Heartbroken, I cried out to God, 'I don't know what to do. Please do something. Save me.' I couldn't tell anyone else; I could only go to God. On one occasion, God spoke, giving me such peace, 'Dawn, this is temporary. It isn't forever.'

"God had competition from alcohol though. By the time I was thirty, addiction numbed all feelings of anxiety and fear.

> *"There is no numbing while exposed to the Lord in moments of prayer. I sat before Him and wept, asking Him the hard questions."*

"In this place of desperation, I came to church with my mother-in-law, who was battling cancer. My spirit was dry and thirsty. I wanted to enter worship but knew my addiction was standing between God and me. I confessed, 'I am so unworthy.'

"I instantly heard God say, 'If you will trust Me, I will burn it away in a minute. I will refine you.' I knew it was Him. When I looked up Scripture about refining later, it always had to do with sin.

"I took God's promise but told Him I wasn't ready. It would be a while before I surrendered and asked Him for help. He never leaves His kids hanging.

> *"He spoke to me so quickly as soon as my heart reached out to Him."*

"When we are willing to lay down our preconceived ideas and approach Him with the faith of a child, He answers. God took the addiction as He promised. I don't need to go to a 12 Step Program to stay sober, but I go to pray for others and care for them."

Kristina experienced God's deep presence as a child, carrying her through times of struggle. Prayer was significant in that season.

"I have such fond memories of Bible camp, where I first received the baptism of the Holy Spirit. I remember when I was in Grade 3, Pastor Don Shea didn't treat us like dumb children: 'Here is the teaching on the Holy Spirit. Here is the baptism.'

"Those were such powerful times. All of the little children were late for *mug up* because the Holy Spirit was upon us and moving mightily.

"As a tender-hearted child, my dad's struggle with alcoholism would break my heart. He would binge drink and suddenly leave our home. As a child, I didn't have a sixth sense and could never predict when he would leave. Almost without fail, however, the Lord would powerfully minister to me before my dad would leave.

"I still look back at camp and those rich times of experiencing God's Presence. I remember my dad had been at home before

193

I left for camp. Then at camp, the Lord met me so beautifully with His Presence. When I got home, my dad was gone. But God's Presence was still so wonderful and tangible.

"When I was in Grade 4, we lived in a small town. As an only child, the journey can be lonelier, especially when there's dysfunction in the home and often only one parent around. Dad had left again because of alcoholism and binge drinking. The tangible Presence of the Lord was so amazing. I would feel the Holy Spirit so strong with me in my little bedroom.

"Sometimes, it's in those hard places, those suffering times, the Lord feels so close and incredibly real. I guess I long for more of His tangible Presence even now when I'm not feeling the depths of suffering."

Allison shared this with me:

"John 14:14 says if we ask anything in Jesus' name, He will do it. If we only tell people God answers every prayer, we've given them half the truth and set them up for failure and shipwreck.

"Everyone needs to know God answers prayer and is unquestionably good and faithful. Sometimes for reasons we don't understand, however, we don't see the answers we hope and believe for. When we fail to teach others about both God's goodness and faithfulness along with the knowledge that He works beyond our understanding, we may hinder people's faith.

"I've heard accusations like, 'How can you say you're a Christian when your life doesn't reflect it? Why are you sick? Why don't you have enough money? Why is your family broken apart, don't you pray? You must have sin in your life.'

"Circumstantial faith lacks the deep roots of knowing God's goodness and faithfulness even if circumstances never change.

If we pray for this one thing every day for the rest of our lives without seeing it come to pass, faith still praises Him believing He can and will do it. We must all aim for deep faith, trusting Him completely no matter what happens.

"I came to the Lord in a word-of-faith type church which taught many absolute truths:

God is good;

He has my best interest in mind;

He is not the Creator of sickness;

He wants us all to prosper in every way and be in health. I'm thankful for that understanding and believe it to be true all the time, even when I don't always see the evidence work out through my prayers.

> *"Is our practice of prayer based on answers to prayer, or based on the character of God?"*

"I want to see the power of God released through prayer. More importantly, I want to know who God is even if I don't see circumstances change. It has been a wrestle for me."

Rae shared about a season of deep suffering.

"I want to start with Psalm 13. Several years into our marriage, everything was extremely painful; marriage was painful; life was painful. I experienced a lot of inner turmoil, was barren and without children. They were years of much pain and journaling. One day, I came across Psalm 13 and threw myself on the floor crying out to God while reading this passage.

'How long, LORD? Will you forget me forever?
How long will you hide your face from me?

How long must I wrestle with my thoughts and day
after day have sorrow in my heart? How long will
my enemy triumph over me?Look on me
and answer, LORD my God. Give light
to my eyes, or I will sleep in death,
and my enemy will say, "I have overcome him,"
and my foes will rejoice when I fall. But I trust in
your unfailing love; my heart rejoices in your
salvation.I will sing the LORD's praise,
For he has been good to me.'

"Mostly I was repeating, 'How long? Will you forget me forever? How long must I wait?'

> *"The Lord took me on a journey with silence and solitude
> —two disciplines I was not familiar with."*

"I had been very much a doer, but God shut me right down. I didn't trust Him and felt like I had a lot of reasons to not trust Him.

"God gave me the grace to step into this season. I was desperate and set aside one day a week, shutting off my phone and answering machine. I would get up and do only what I had to do to prepare for the day and then go lay on the couch. I would lay there until the Lord told me to do something, whether that was to go for a walk, vacuum my floors or whatever.

"I battled with my flesh because everything inside of me thought this was crazy. I felt lazy and guilty for not doing more. Week after week, this is what I did. The Lord took me through a time of fasting—fasting from friendships and fasting from looking at myself in the mirror. I felt like I was getting stripped. It was all out of obedience to Him.

"One day, God told me to take a blanket and put it over top of myself. When I did, He said, 'The weight of My glory is like the weight of this blanket.'

196

"It was like I could physically feel the weight. I remember kneeling on the floor with the blanket over my head in a posture of worship. I could only stay there for a few minutes. The glory was too much for me. I felt so afraid, uncomfortable, and unworthy.

"Looking back, I can see how that time affected me. I'm still drawn to the weight of His glory. It's not in the same way it was then, but I would say God showed Himself to me as the Lover of my soul. I would have evenings where I'd turn off all the lights in my house, light candles, play worship music, and just worship and talk to Him.

> *"During a really hard time, God brought me into a journey of intimacy I had never known or experienced before."*

"Shortly afterward, we sold our tiny house and moved to where we are now. We took on an enormous responsibility in owning a property with a rental in it. Three years after moving here, rain flooded us out. Because our primary living space was in the basement, our home was ruined. Without sufficient resources or finances, it was a seven-year journey of restoration. Through that time, I got back into the doing mode again, was committed to children's ministry, and started a business. I was also experiencing the trauma of the destruction of my home and reliving the horror of my past.

"Suddenly, all these memories started coming back. All the years before, I often said to my husband, 'I wonder if I've been raped.' I had so much fear and anger, internally knowing.

"I had a remembrance of an incident where my mom was attacked and her attacker saying to me, 'Little girl, you better run or you're next.' I ran out into the yard. Miraculously, my dad had not yet left to go out to the field.

"As God brought back brief memories, I felt I needed to confirm with my parents and ask if they were real. They verified I had been raped and my mom was attacked. I was probably two or three years old at the time and ran out into the yard.

"At first, it felt like the skeleton was out of the closet and there was a genuine sense of relief, but I didn't have an emotional connection to any of it. Then my health started to go. I experienced fatigue in a way I hadn't known before and didn't understand. I didn't know what was going on.

"Around the same time, a group of us went down to Kansas City to the International House of Prayer (IHOP). I met a lady there, who, by the grace of God, dove into the depth of my mess and understood it all. She told me, 'Rae, when things get hard, message me and just say, "Pray." I'm on it.'

"The next day, we were in the prayer room at IHOP and suddenly, the floodgates of emotions rose within me. I didn't know what to do with them.

"That took me on a year-long journey. I would find myself in heaves. All I would do is message her saying, 'Pray,' and she would respond. I don't know what I would have done without her and her prayers.

"I experienced adrenal fatigue and went on a journey of health and wellness, had a nutritional coach, shut down my business, and wasn't doing Kingdom Kids anymore. I worked two-and-a-half days a week for five years at a flooring store; that's all I could handle.

"Today, I have my health back. I am running up to five kilometers at a time. It's a real joy. God is so good. He has proven Himself to be so faithful. He really is the Lover of my soul. There are still healing things that have to happen, but during one inner healing, God had me do the same thing with a blanket. When the session was over both the facilitator and my husband said, 'Who are you? Your face is even different.'

"I still ask, 'Really, Lord, how long?'

"We've been married for twenty-two years this August and still don't have children. Yet, as hard as that is, I wouldn't trade the journey I've gone on with God and the healing of my soul, mind and body. He healed my broken heart. He healed my health. I wouldn't trade those things for the world. I once had a rage I couldn't deal with and no self-control. As hard as not having children is, I feel like I have so much.

"I still believe I will have children someday, but they'll have a mother who is a whole person. For that, I'm thankful.

"When I was nineteen and in Bible school, God put it into my heart to become the woman He created me to be. I had no idea this would be the journey He would take me on. Even though there is so much more to the process, I feel like I can say today I'm the woman He created me to be.

"He is faithful!

> **"They overcame him by the blood of the Lamb and**
> **by the word of their testimony, and they did not**
> **love their lives to the death."**
> **Revelation 12:11 (NKJV)**

Perhaps the worst tragedy to happen to a family is the death of a child. Second Kings 4:8-36 tells of a Shunammite woman's gracious hospitality to Elisha, a powerful prophet. She built a special room for him in her home, so he could enjoy the best of accommodations when in the area.

Though she asked for nothing in return, Elisha wanted to reward her. Since she was childless, he said, **"About this time next year . . . you will hold a son in your arms"**(2 Kgs 4:16).

Though the dream of bearing a child died long ago, within a year

God's promise was fulfilled as she held her baby boy. Nothing marked his childhood as unusual. Then one day while in the field with his father, the boy's head began to ache. Before the sun had set, the child died in his mother's arms.

She took no time to grieve, and without hesitation laid his small body on the prophet's bed. Without telling even her husband the seriousness of the events, she mounted a donkey and quickly rode off to find Elisha. God promised a son, born from a dead womb; only God could raise a dead son back to promise. Though the journey took many hours, she was unwavering in her faith.

When she found him, the Shunammite refused to leave Elisha's side. Elisha immediately sent his servant ahead to pray for the boy. With unshakable faith, she believed this man of God alone could reverse death's grip and restore life's sure embrace. Another arduous day's journey passed before they reached home.

Alone in the room with the small corpse, Elisha interceded again and again. His prayers were not in vain; the boy was restored to his mother alive and well.

> *"When I pray, I know God is sovereign. He is King! He is a powerful Father who cares." – Christie*

The Shunammite woman's story perfectly illustrates the power of persistent faith and believing prayer. Many others have infused their prayers with the same tenacity, yet with the opposite effect.

Why? Why was God's promise fulfilled and then seemingly stolen? Why did this family have to go through such intense sorrow to find equally intense joy? As we keep reading the story, we find God had a greater purpose for the death of her son and the suffering she endured.

Shortly after, Elisha warned the Shunammite of an approaching seven-year famine (2 Kgs 8:1-6). Without hesitation, she packed their few belongings and sought refuge in the land of the Philistines. In her absence, however, her home and land were confiscated. At the end of the famine, she returned appealing to the king to have her property returned.

"Just as Gehazi was telling the king how Elisha

> had restored the dead to life, the woman whose
> son Elisha had brought back to life came to appeal
> to the king for her house and land . . . This is the
> woman, my lord the king, and this is her son whom
> Elisha restored to life."
> **2 Kings 8:5**

God's timing is always perfect. At the precise moment Elisha's servant was telling the king about the resurrection miracle, the living evidence entered the room. Immediately, the king assigned a special official to her case, restoring everything back to her: home, land, and all the earnings from the land during her absence. Who but God could orchestrate such things?

If there had never been a death,
> there would never have been a resurrection,
>> a king would never hear the miraculous story,
>>> a widow's home would never be restored,
>> her land would never have been secured, and
> finances would never have been provided.

Lowell and Staci, like the Shunammite, discovered God's sovereignty through struggle. God's plans and purposes are far greater than any present problem. After years of barrenness, this woman refused to be denied when tragedy struck. She trusted her situation to God alone. When all hope faded and everything seemed lost, her faith rested not in the promise of God, but with the God of promise. There, and there alone, she found her help.

Other sons have died without being brought back to life. Crises have gripped godly people without answers or restitution. It begs the question, "Why?" What do we do then?

I'll let Kevin answer.

"We can choose to be Kingdom sighted or short-sighted. To be short-sighted is situational and circumstantial.

"Just a short while ago, my grandsons were born prematurely —one stillborn, the other thriving. 'God, how can this be?' I asked, 'I know You are good in both these situations.'

"I finished holding my deceased grandson, praying he would come to life. He didn't. Then I stood in neonatal praying for my grandson who was thriving. I was upset because I had prayed asking God for long life for both of them. 'Lord, how is this possible. Your Word tells me in both these situations You are good.'

"The first thing God reminded me was that He didn't cause harm to either of my grandsons. The second thing He spoke was, 'Will you choose to be Kingdom sighted in the difficult situation you have been through? Will you endeavor to see and find my heart here?'

"Because I was so upset, I said, 'No!'

"I realized if I'm *not* willing to be Kingdom sighted about everything going on in my life and around me, I stay stuck in short-sightedness. Becoming hard-hearted will not allow me to understand the power of prayer. I want to pursue Kingdom-sighted prayer, which goes from generation to generation."

Unmasking the Myth

No barrier feels more insurmountable than the apparent silence of God. Even with hearts sensitive and tuned to the frequencies of Heaven, it's difficult to constantly recognize His Presence. In times of struggle, it's easy to believe the myth that God is distant, distracted, uninterested, or preoccupied.

When the sword of pain and loss cuts its ugly sweep across our lives, what truth holds firm? What foundation remains unshake-able? How does faith stand strong then? In our unanswered attempts, we ask, 'Is this prayer?'"

Biblical truth remains the unshakeable foundation of all truth. Feelings rise and fall moment by moment, but the Word of God is the
anchor securing our swaying ship,
light shining through our darkest hour,
true north directing our unmarked path,
hope for our hopelessness,
help for our helplessness,
strength for our weariness,
power guiding our feeblest prayer.

> *"In the hard places, He shows Himself as our everything." – Emily*

Over and over, the Bible declares God is with us. He is closer than we imagine. Truth repudiates the lies of the enemy. The psalmist, David, wrote,

> **"The Lord is close to all whose hearts are crushed**
> **by pain, and he is always ready to restore**
> **the repentant one."**
> **Psalm 34:18 TPT**

By embracing biblical truth, we discover our hearts follow in faith, if ever so slowly. When faith feels absent or too weak to matter, a mustard seed portion is enough to move the immoveable in our lives (Mt 17:20).

The myth surrounding God's silence declares God's indifference to our suffering. This lie takes root in the shallow soil of our misunder-standing about the nature, character, and goodness of God. It's in the rocky ground of unknowing that the lie of the enemy thrives.

During the seasons of my greatest despair, God seemed so very distant. Only later did I realize He was nearer than I dreamed, doing His greatest work in the deepest areas of my heart.

Like an Artist retreating to His studio, in the place of struggle

God quietly perfects a masterpiece of our lives. Like a skillful Author, He turns the pages of our hearts, writing His glorious story upon the soft flesh of brokenness.

> *"One of the first things I heard God say to me was, 'This was never the life I had for you. I have cried so many tears for you.' That shook me!"*
> *— Shelly*

As we press into God during times of deep struggle, pushing past the numbness, we find Him faithful. God's nearness remains constant; He is only a breath away.

"The LORD is near to all who call on him,
to all who call on him in truth."
Psalm 145:18

The psalmists emphatically declare there is no place we could go where God is not already present (Ps 139:7-12). Luke wrote, **"He is not far from any one of us"** (Acts 17:27).

> *"God, I cannot see or hear You at this moment. My emotions are raw; my heart is torn open. I ask You to circle me with Your love. Open the eyes of my heart to sense Your Presence again and the ears of my spirit to hear the words You are speaking at this moment. I give You the brokenness of all I am. May I become increasingly sensitive to Your nearness. I declare my love for You and rest waiting for Your love to cocoon me in this season."*

"We say with confidence our prayers are answered
because we know we are praying to God
who cares for us."
— Mike

***

"Just pray! Then pray some more! Pray through
the discouragements, frustrations, persecutions,
fears, and laziness. Pray!"
— Sharon

***

"When my heart was broken, I would press into God
through worship on the piano. His Presence
would seep into all the cracks in me,
healing the broken places."
— Amanda C.

Epilogue

Undeniably prayer leads us to awe-inspiring, mountain-top victories, and equally deep valleys of uncertainty. It is a journey of unparalleled faith and trust. Yet, the most fulfilling relational expedition one could ever experience in partnership with God.

The worst thing that could happen now for this book, and the voices echoing within its pages, is to be placed on a shelf—discounted and forgotten. Resist the temptation to nullify the life experiences of those who have shared their perspectives. Rather than reserved for a select few, the path of prayer—God's gift of grace—lays open for us all.

Jeremiah 33:3 has been the guiding verse for this prayer project; its theme has woven a continuous thread of strength throughout each testimony.

> **"Call to me and I will answer you and tell you great**
> **and unsearchable things you do not know."**

Prayer, though often perceived as boring, will be anything but dull, when wrapped within a living relationship with the Father, Son and Holy Spirit.

"Great and unsearchable things," (NIV)
  "remarkable secrets," (NLT)[1]
    "great and mighty things," (KJV)
      "wonderful and marvelous things," (GNT)[2]
        await the people of prayer.

Those who have shared their experiences welcome you to join them in this wonderful journey of prayer.

Notes:

1. Tyndale House Publishers. 2004. Holy Bible: New Living Translation. Wheaton, Ill: Tyndale House Publishers.
2. American Bible Society. 1976. Good news Bible: the Bible in Today's English version. New York: American Bible Society.

Special Thanks

No words can express the deep gratitude and thanks due to my
husband and family. Without your love and support,
the pen would sit idle and pages void.
Love and appreciate you all!

Author Bio

Wife, mother and grandmother; mentor and friend; author, teacher
and speaker; servant of many; farm girl always;
lover of Jesus forever.
Many hats worn by the same woman
who loves the simple
pleasures of family and friends,
stopping by unexpected
and sleeping over without invitation.
There's nothing like a quiet day
sitting on the slopes
of the Qu'Appelle Valley,
lazing in the backyard listening to birds,
or casting a line in a nearby lake fishing.
God's gifts to a grateful heart.

Contact

https://maward.ca/about-maryann-ward/

ReMade Ministries
Box 205
Balgonie, Saskatchewan, CA
S0G 0E0

maryann@maward.ca

Other Books By

Unlocking Legacy the second book gleaned from dozens of interviews explores further aspects of prayer, such as: humility, fasting, prophecy, creativity, travailing, intercession and more. *Unlocking Legacy* gives strategies for possessing our godly inheritance through prayer. Each chapter contains miraculous accounts of God's grace.
Published 2020

Olivia & Me, a children's picture book, presenting the truth of John 10:10, **"I have to come that they may have life, and have it to the full."** Through a parallel journey between a little girl and a caterpillar turned butterfly, *Olivia & Me* illustrates life **"to the full."** On earth and in heaven.
Published 2017